AF378472

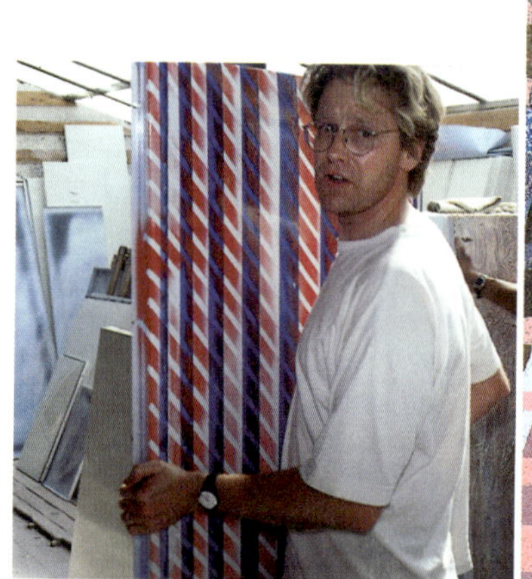

1

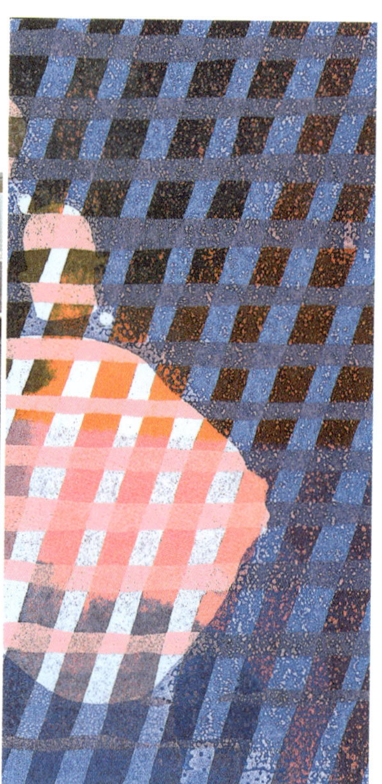

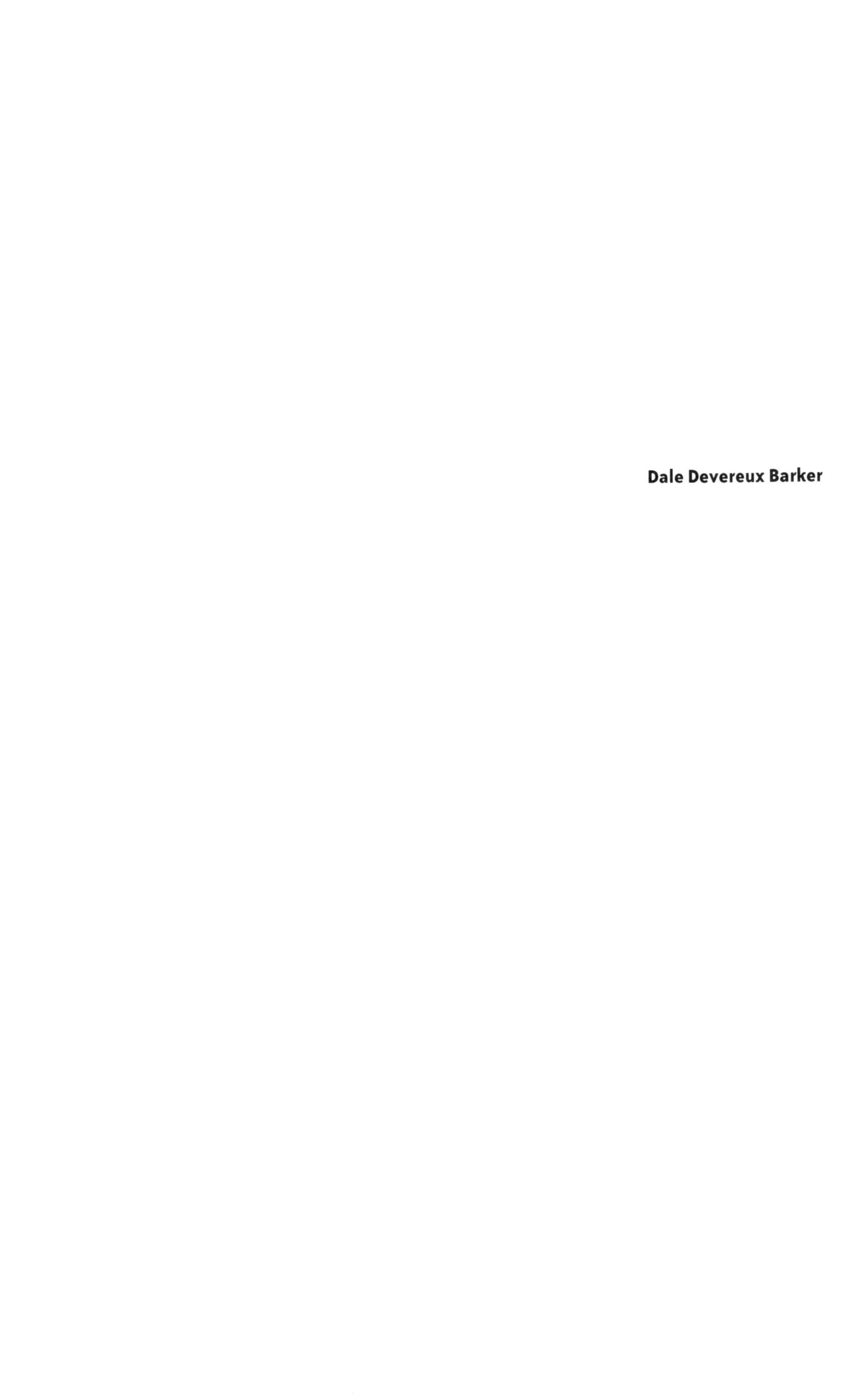

Dale Devereux Barker

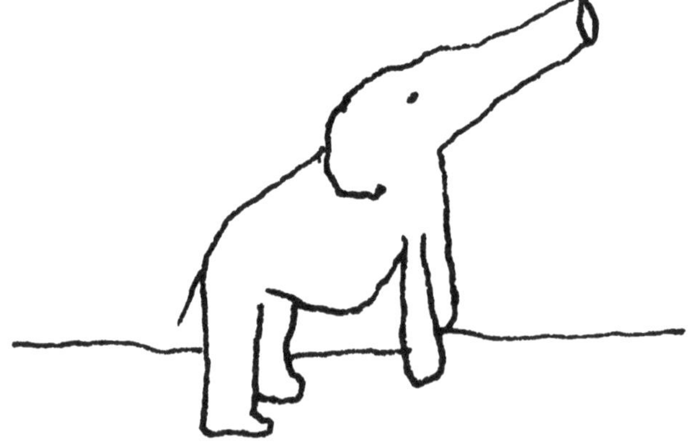

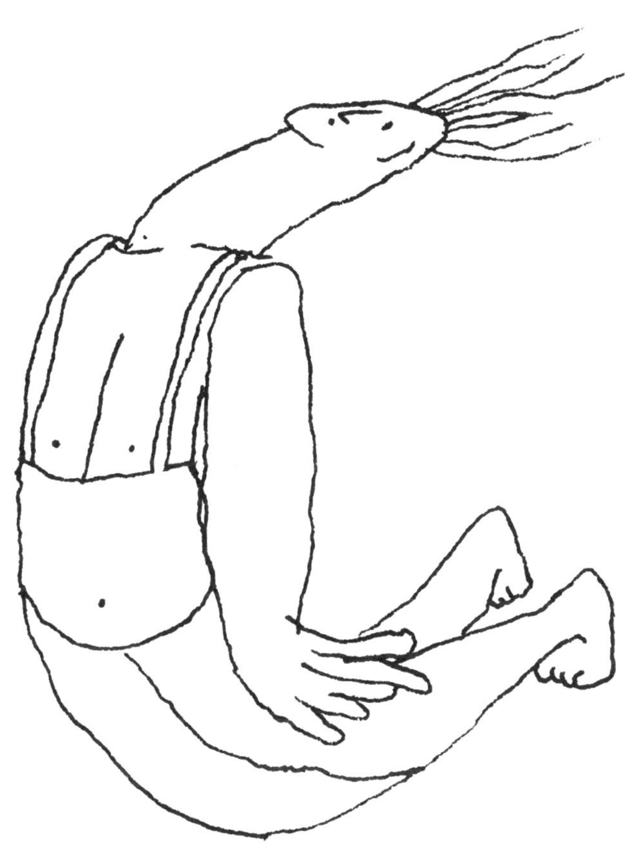

Acknowledgments

(for Dale)

The artist and author wish to express their gratitude to the
publications in which these collaborations originally
appeared: 'Particeps Criminis': TransAtlantic News;
'Disgruntled Lug': Science and Wonder; 'Forbidden Rhymes':
Psychology Today; 'A Sable Figure Cloaked in Gloom Told Us
This Hilarious Joke': Psychological Digest; 'Killer Abstractions':
Modern Psychology; 'You Don't Remember Us, Do You?':
Psychology Review; 'Poem Contaminated by Prepositions':
Times Literary Supplement; 'Elegy for the Split Infinitive':
New England Journal of Medicine; 'For the Development of the
Split Infinitive': The Wall Street Journal; 'To Our Esteemed
Selves': Humanities Quarterly; 'Oliver Happily Totals His
Cadillac': Dactyls on Parade; 'The Case Against The Gullible
Pagans': The Journal of Theological Studies; 'Our Friend,
The Adverb': Materials Management Weekly; 'Excellent Sonnet
to a Nymph': Hunters and Gatherers Quarterly.

And our special thanks to Haiku Annual for a Special Mention
Certificate in The Dubious Theme Category for 'Collaborative
Effort That Extols the Pleasures of Urban Life While
Gratuitously Employing at Least Five Annoyingly Obscure
Words and the Image of an Overturned Barrel of Olives on a
Rain-glazed Cobblestone Street.'

Paul Violi

This is the first extensive publication to explore
Dale Devereux Barker's work. It charts his
development to date and gives an insight into his
lively and very unique palette. Dale has exhibited
predominantly in the medium of print both
nationally and internationally over the past
fifteen years. His versatility and inventive
approach has earned him a reputation as much
for large scale outdoor commissions for the
corporate client as for collaborations with poets,
writers and artists in an international arena.
It is refreshing and energising to work with Dale
who is examining ideas of the maker and role of
the artist today, especially now, as we pause for
thought at the start of a new century.

Katherine Wood
Firstsite
December 1999

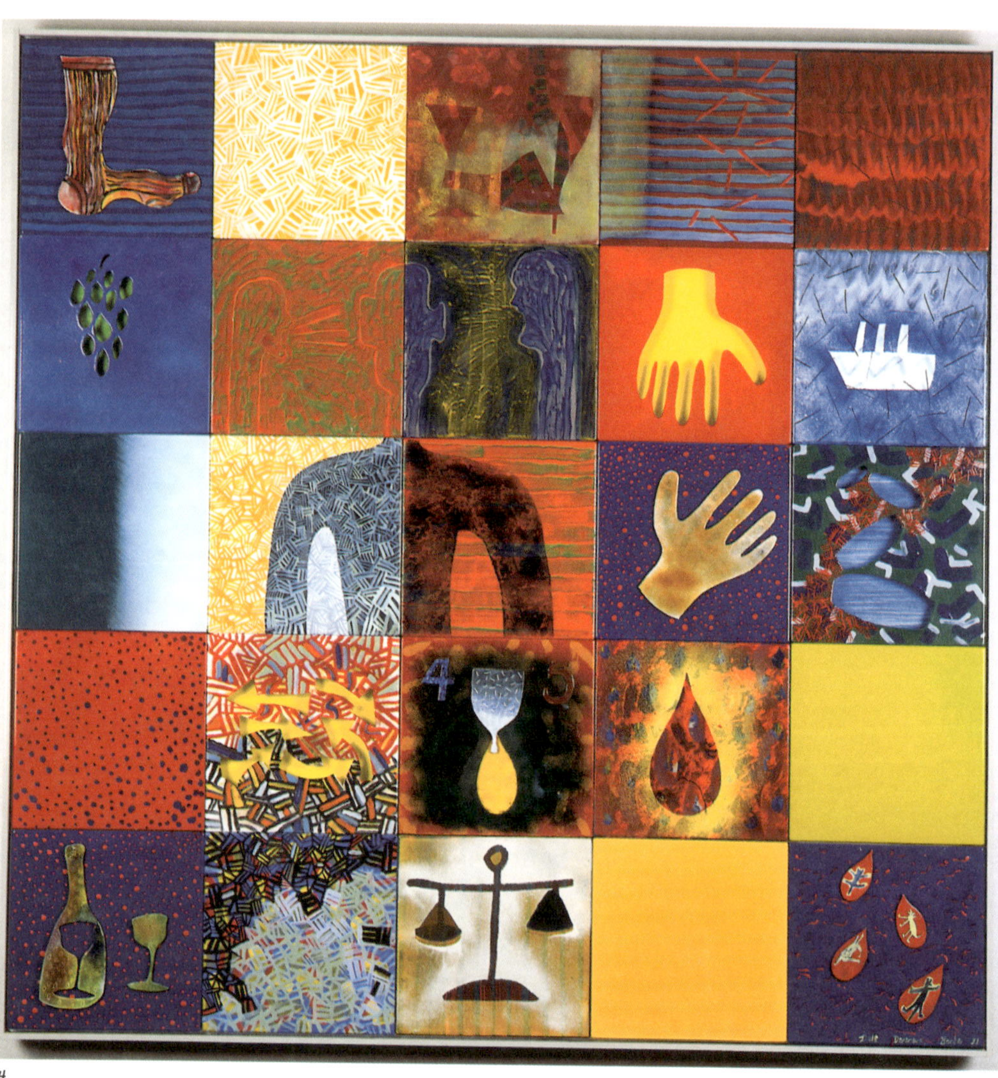

4

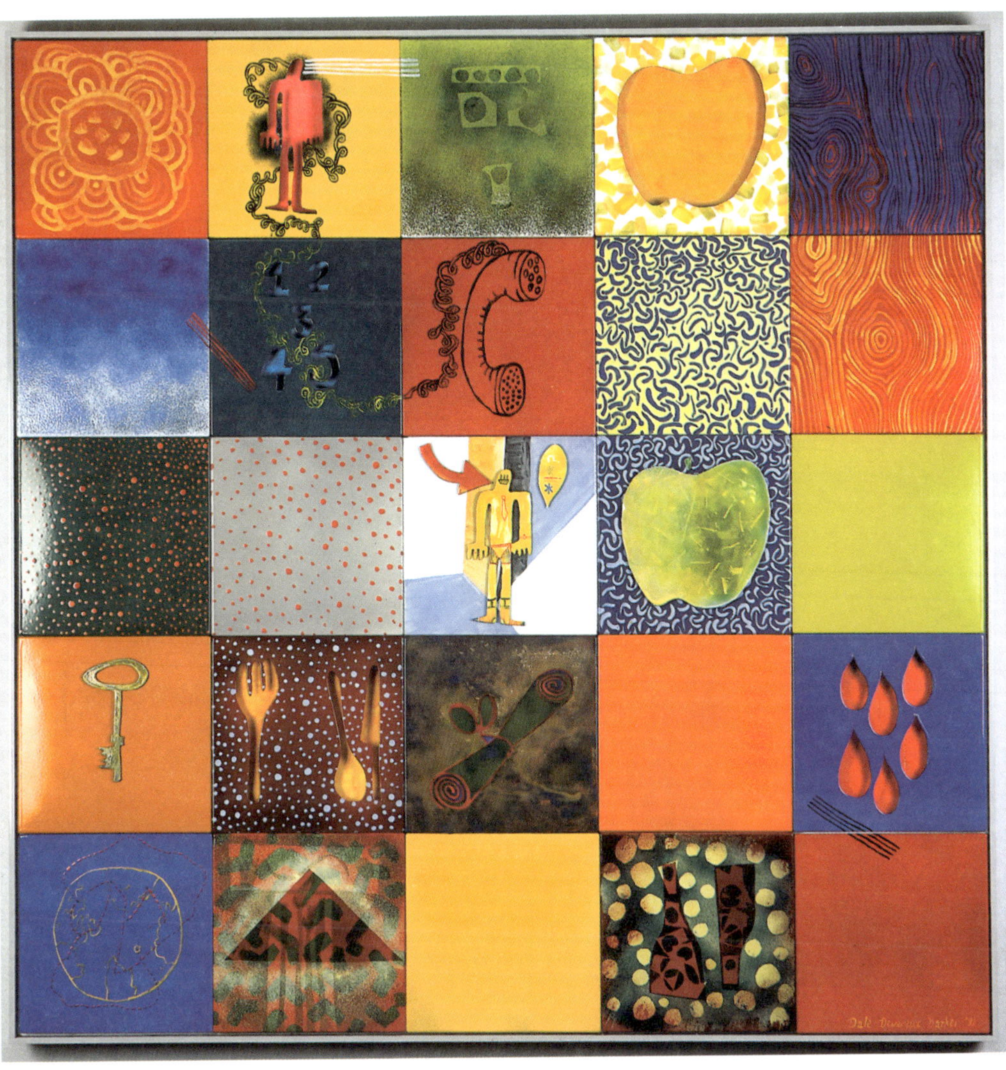

5

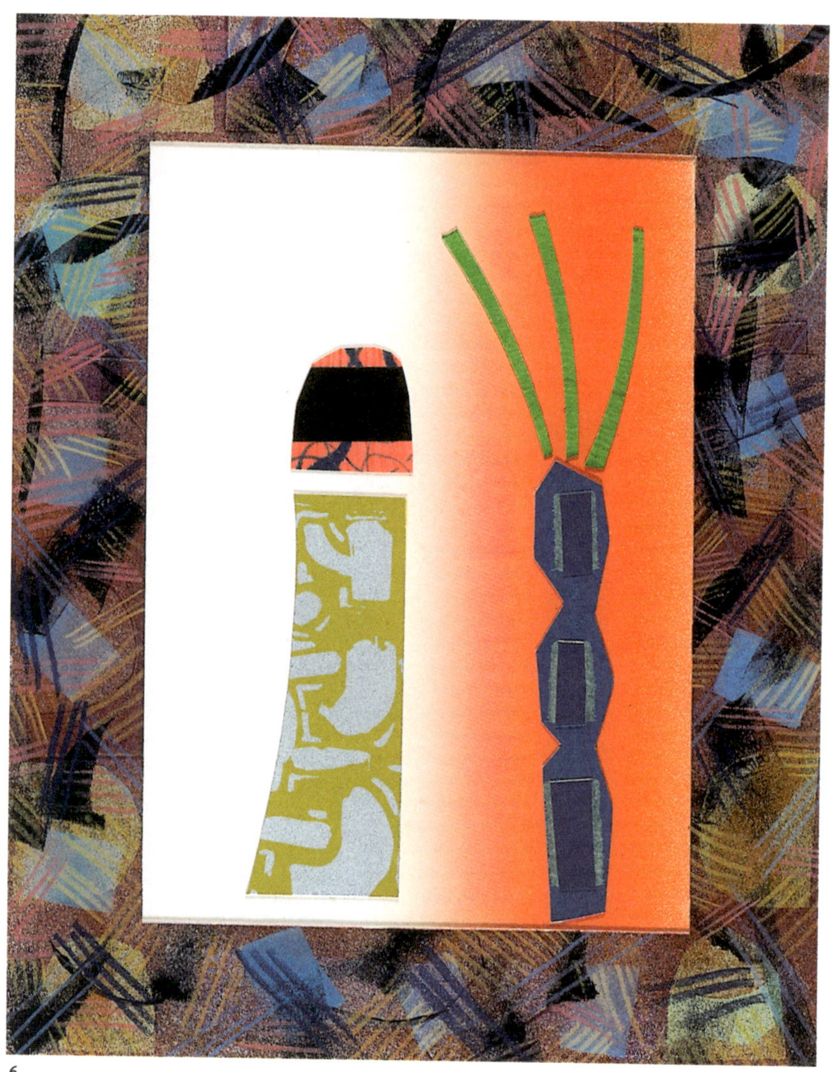

6

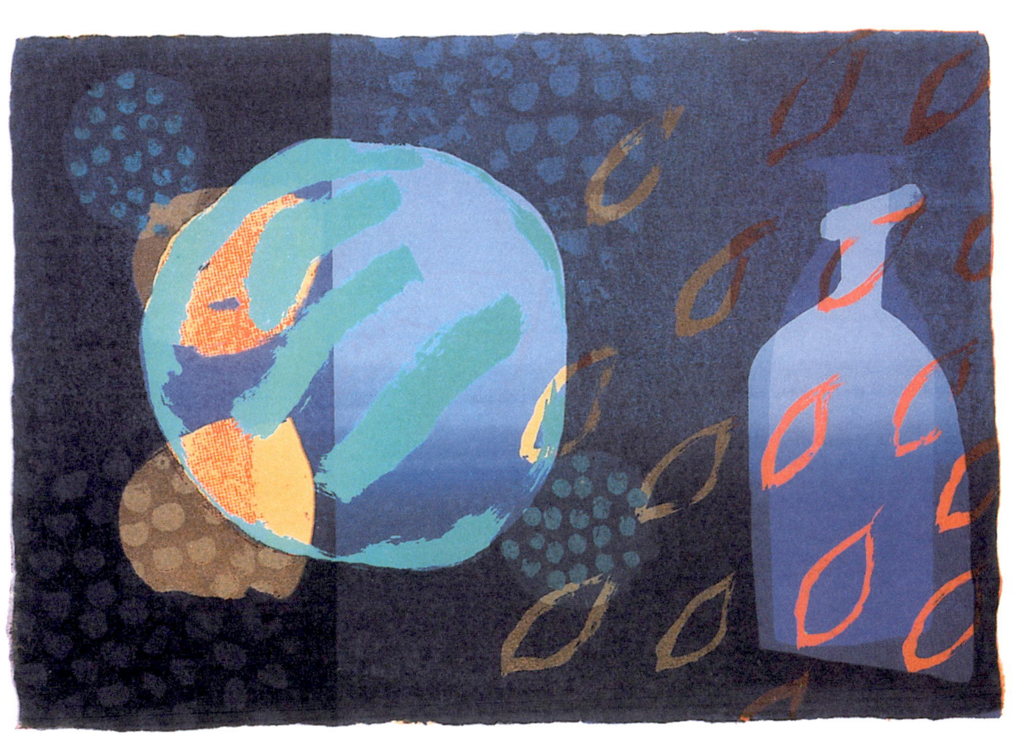

7

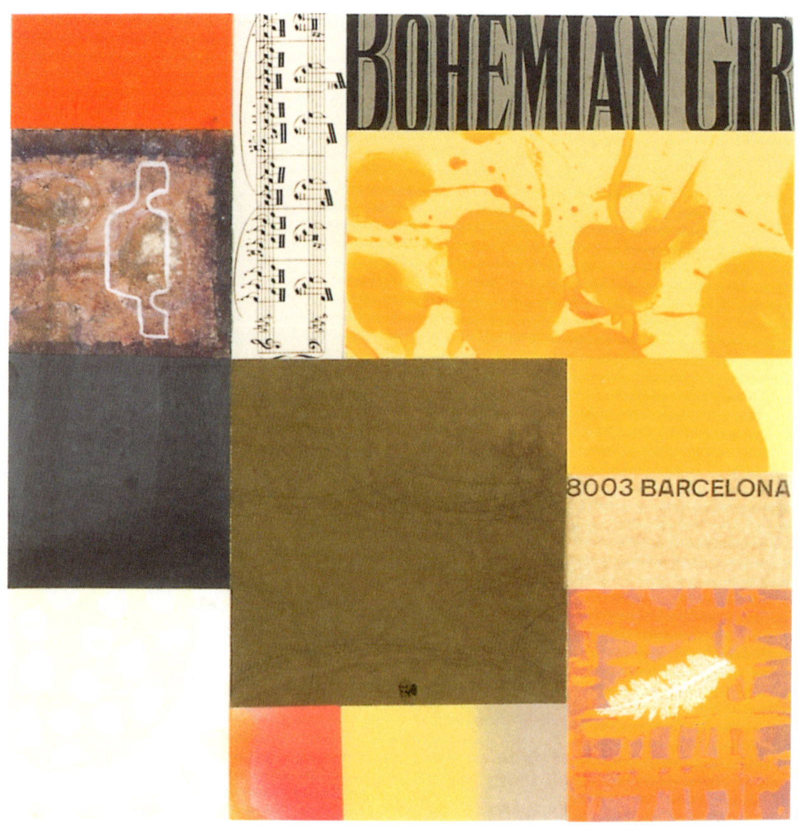

8

What does one make pictures out of?

Emma Hill

The question is posed in relation to a small black and white lino print. The image, though simple, takes time to interpret and with the benefit of hindsight I risk describing it as a flying bottle, or at least a bottle-like object which definitely has wings. Around the print is a hand drawn border of blue flowers. The image is contained in a rough bound book, little more than a sequence of one-block linos with text hand written by the artist, some prints animated by the addition of coloured doodles, most left plain. The title appears in faded letraset: *Things that Fly*.

In another one-off volume of art school juvenilia the artist has assembled various pairings of pictures (cut out from magazines, photographs, photocopies, fragments of etchings) with printed texts apparently culled from old lexicons and encyclopaedias of ephemera. The surreal juxtapositions are dark and funny, some potentially deep, others irreverently inconsequential.

Dale Devereux Barker makes art out of all sorts of things: out of pictures, out of words, out of humour, out of frustration, out of sex, out of sitting on the beach. Since graduating from the Slade in 1986 he has developed a pictorial language which is distinctive in its combination of figurative imagery and complex layering of more abstract planes and textures scavenged from outside sources. Barker is a dexterous practitioner and the work at its best carries a sense of ease that belies the complexity of its technical process. He has the ability to use various media within the same image to load up the references, or to present an observation with the bold shorthand of a Keith Haring. Barker's language is accessible and often extremely seductive – be it the plays of

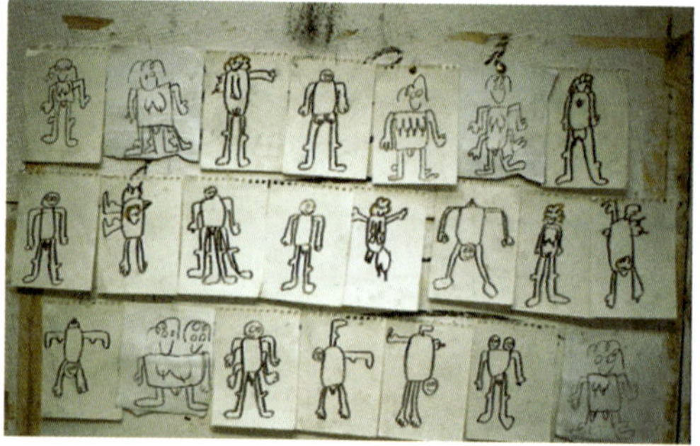

9

density and depth in the screened perspex prints, the glistening surfaces of the enamel panels, the combination of computer generated plates, etchings and hand worked prints in the most recent bookworks or the tiny, hand sewn unique editions – jewel-like in their colours, fragments from a larger whole.

Barker makes it look simple, even throwaway sometimes, but what emerges in an examination of the work of the last ten years is the coherent development of a serious artist.

A single flower sprouts from a hilltop, it's roots depicted in the bisected ground beneath; a shower fixing cascades water into an empty room; a figure is isolated in a hallucinatory background of fragmenting elements; a dinosaur strolls against the silhouette of a rising planet. The images carry a curious poignancy, which is both funny and fragile. Barker makes art out of the randomness of things, out of curious moments isolated pictorially.

Drawing in time and
in the time between
the conversation
with the thing out there
and what it seemed to me [1]

Dale Devereux Barker's work has always implied a strong sense of narrative. Early single images were often attached to oblique lines of text or developed in sequences of related prints (see the sequence of swimming prints). An early bookwork, *The Legacy* 1989, was described by Stanley Jones as 'a unified object… offered for contemplation' where an aperture cut into the green leather binding presented a series of ten

10

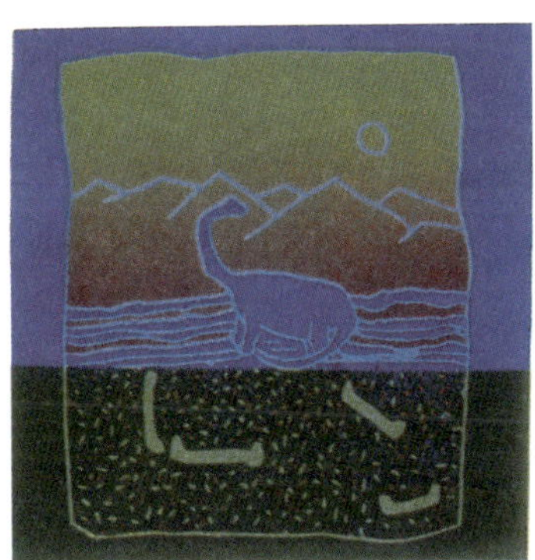

11

tiny linos. Horizon lines within these minute images gave the work an ambiguous scale. They depicted for the most part emptied out landscapes, their titles and anonymous subjects creating an oblique but evocative commentary on the central notion of man's legacy for the future world. In other prints of the early 1990s objects, figures and decorative motifs were arranged in grids of multi-coloured squares or took on a kind of animation when isolated out in a single image. Scales jumped within the same picture plane, creating a sense of illogical but hermetic space within the images. Colours were often applied in peculiar combinations, darker tones given resonance by more brilliant underprinting.

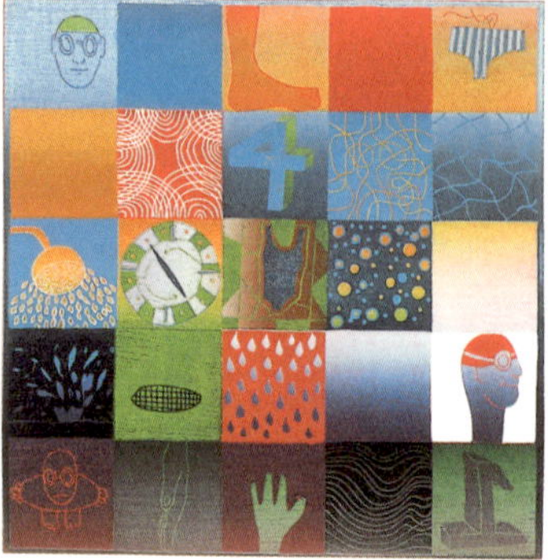

12

The particular line of the linocut, how it bites into the hard but spongy surface of the block has, I think, had an enormous influence over how Barker's drawing has evolved and how it is he thinks through the finished image from the first or bottom-most layer of the print. The sense of being able to isolate the singular by graphic means and to build up texture or gradate colour across an inked, rolled surface or translate depth into layers of screened perspex, comes from these early reduction-method lino prints. The threads of this early work are still present – his recent installation at the Eagle Gallery (London February 1999) centred on a montage of over 200 fragments – individual, mixed media works on paper which were in essence the sketches towards a bookwork *The Hazards of Imagery*. These miniatures were drawn, printed, letterpressed, collaged, painted, found, assembled. Some were simply type blocks of random letters, others tiny, peopled vignettes. Some images stood complete, others were so oblique they became more like textures playing over the whole. The piece read from a distance as

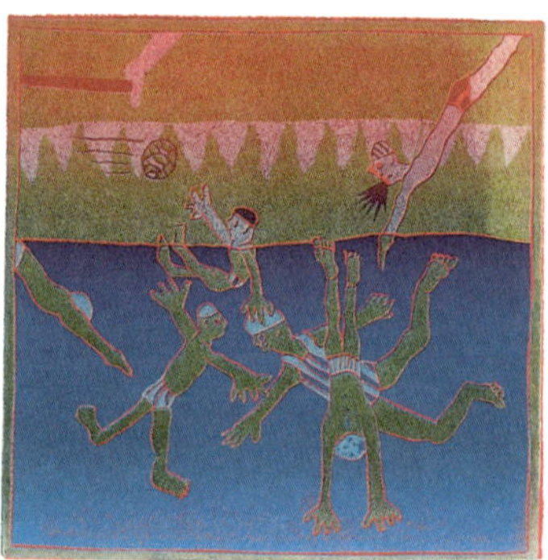

13

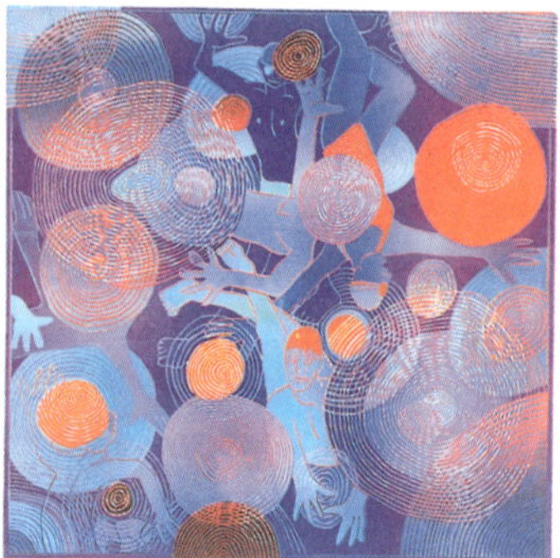

15

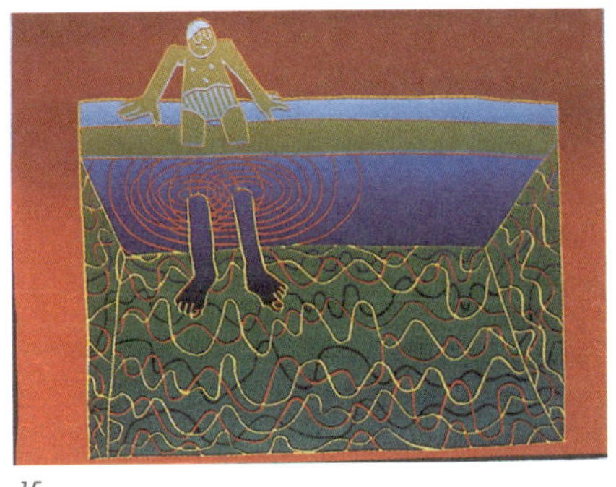

15

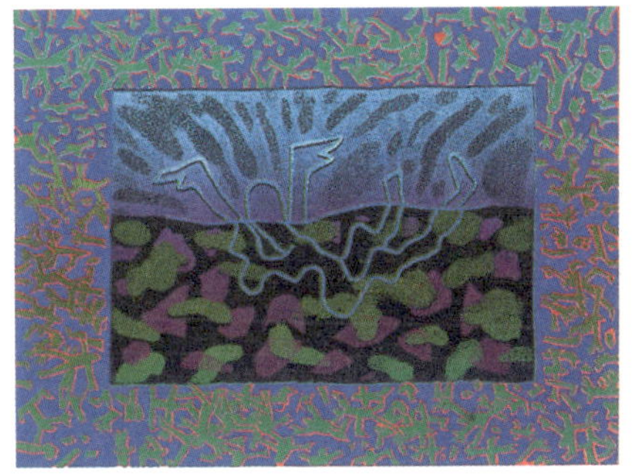

16

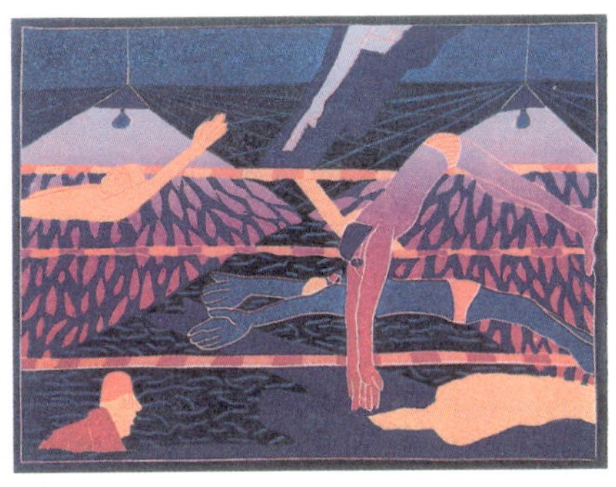

17

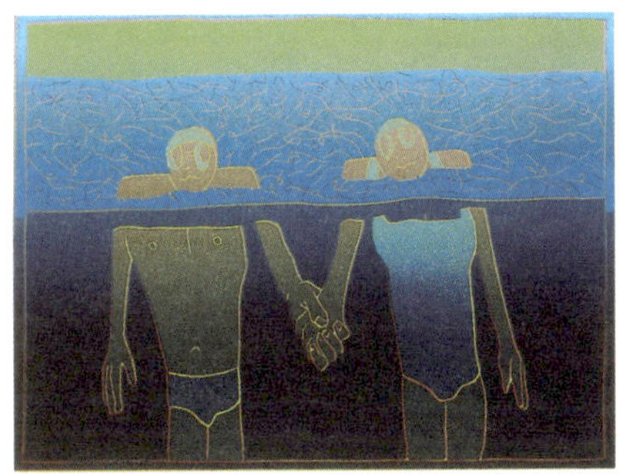

18

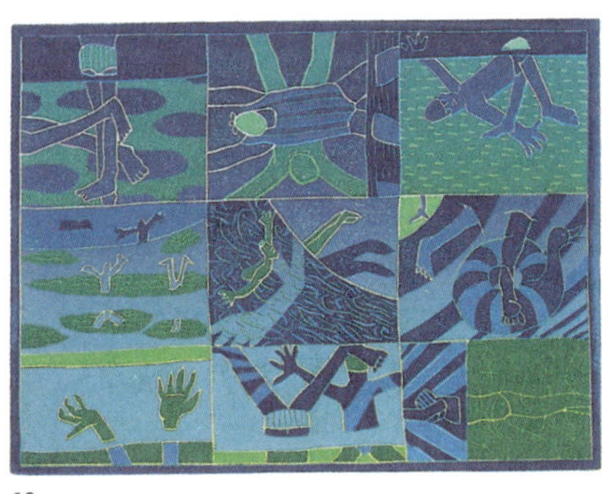

19

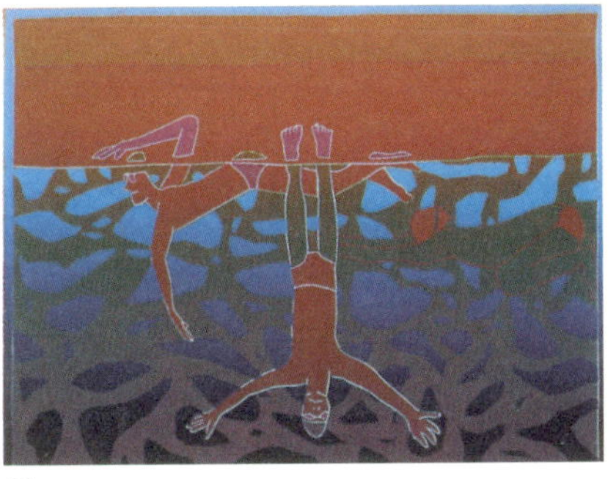

20

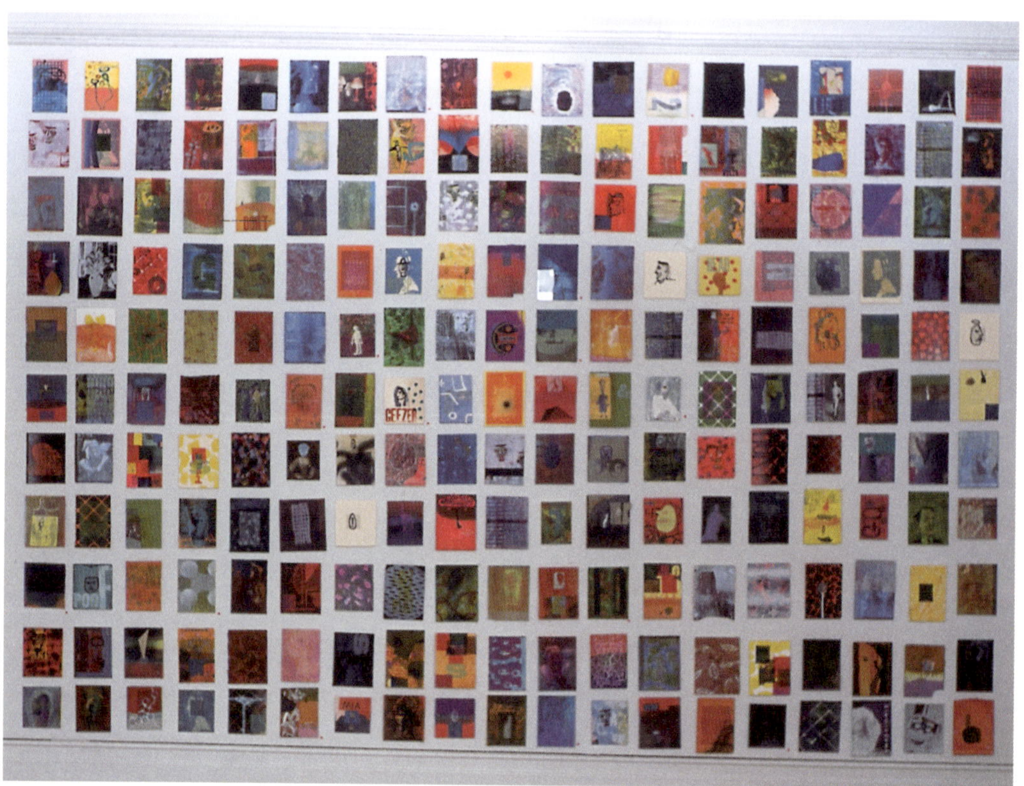

21

a rich, monumental painting, but close to, one became involved in trying to decipher the curious visual stories that arose in the juxtapositions of the different pictures.

The work had a random chaotic energy – the sense that one was looking at an enormous on-going visual diary, collaged from arbitrary moments in one individual's consciousness. It worked abstractly, in that no one image was given precedence over another, yet set up curious visual and contextual patterns in the repetitions of differently worked versions of the same printed images or snippets of text. As a counterpoint to this tapestry of unedited ideas the bookwork had a more formal austerity – a confidence to pare down the images in a way that allowed the particular clarity of Paul Violi's poems to function both as text but also integrated as image into the whole.

Early in 1989, Barker and I began an exchange of texts and images following discussions about how his pictures implied to me a succession of individual stories or pictorial shorthand. His challenge to 'write me some words' led to a two-year collaboration and resulted ultimately in *The Dreaming Side*. The subject of the book was to an extent a reflection on what had led us both to make things. We wanted to produce a work that spoke about the imagination, about colour, about memory. We wanted an equal balance between words and images, so that neither was simply illustrative of the other. We wanted to produce an object, which gave a sense of quality from the moment one touched the page, and to use the fast disappearing technique of letterpress to give weight to the treatment of the texts. The long discussions we had about design, type, paper and

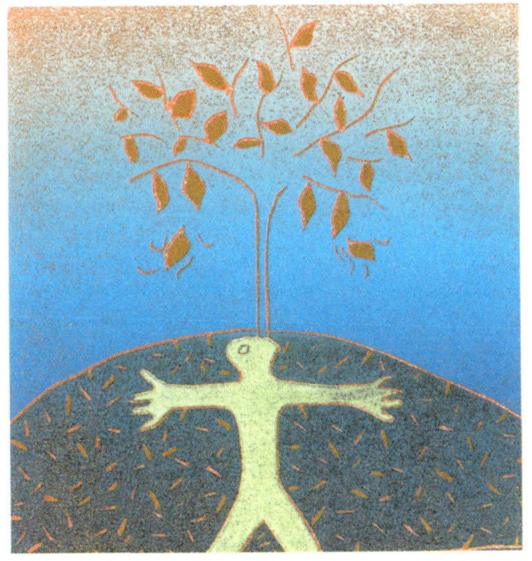

22

binding resulted in a book which is more graphically formal than any bookworks Barker has made since. *The Dreaming Side* is close to the traditional notion of the *livre d'artist* with single images and related texts held within bound folio pages. There is no narrative connection between the sections but the sequence has a particular progression and formal decisions about colour and image stemmed from this. The book rises and falls away in a sense, starting from a simple black and white image about sleep and passing through a series of observations about love, nature and dreaming. All of the prints were made by hand, with each new layer cut from the same lino block. The process involved a great deal of labour and the risk that whole sections could be lost through a single mistake in the printing. What it gives the book is a sense that, though editioned, each copy is in some way unique, whether it is the change of tone in a background colour or the mis-registration of a block along an edge. The texts stemmed in part from quite literal memories of particular events – a storm in Germany, swimming at night off the coast of Scotland, gathering summer fruit; and attempted to pinpoint these moments that remain in the consciousness. It is this clarity of recollection, this moment of individual memory that somehow becomes universal which Barker is able to capture in his images.

Life's little loops
Life's stupid ironies
Life's comic cuts
Life's dead ends
Life's open heart surgeries
Life's great chip shop closed when you're hungry [2]

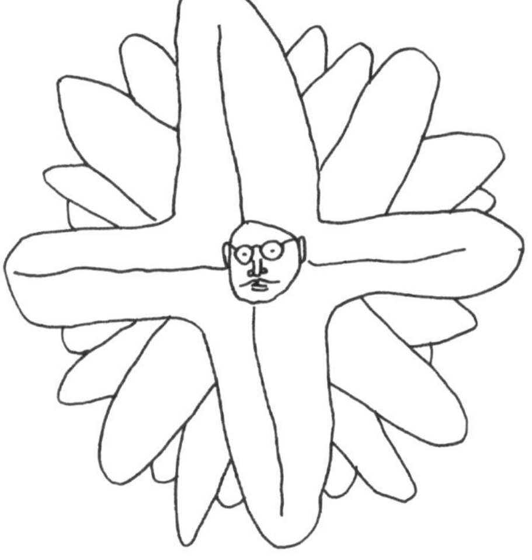

23

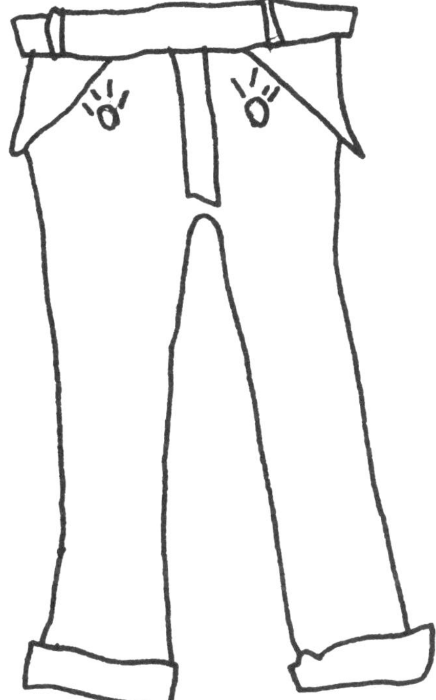

Barker has continued to use words in the various bookworks he has made alongside his practice as a painter and printmaker. They are another tool and have informed the development of his work in many ways. The breadth of pictorial references in the recent prints, the intrusions of computer collaged imagery and pixilated texture seem directly related to the acerbic and visually loaded poems of Paul Violi. The recurrent use of typescript, with its jumpy spacing and utilitarian design, stems from working with Martin Stannard's ironic poem *From a Recluse to A Roving I Will Go* and is refined in the shimmering silver texts of *The Hazards of Imagery* or intrudes upon and breaks up the glossy, decorative surfaces of the new monoprints.

On a practical level an increased awareness of type and of the grid that underpins good textual design has led Barker to edit and refine his images with increasing confidence. Often an effect is heightened by a punctuation or pause and it is as if Barker has learned to pace himself through the process of book making and extends this now to the placing of the different elements that make up his images. The writers that he has worked with in recent years share a kind of matter-of-factness in their approach. More importantly they share a humane, inventive humour, for Barker has never lost the ability to highlight the incongruous and the absurd in his visual commentary on the world.

Under the Boardwalk

Down by the sea
is a shop where one can purchase
an inflatable pope.
Inflatable saints, warriors,
luscious heroines and winged kings,
martyrs, triumphant crusaders,
and, for a slightly higher price,
the most inspiring philosophers
are also available.
Made by local artisans,
their features are truly lifelike,
truly cuddlesome, their sturdiness
and reliability guaranteed.
The people adore them.
They float on them in fountain pools
or moor them to their rooftops.
When strong winds blow
some choose to tie a bunch
of their favorites together
and grasping the lines as if holding
the most illustrious bouquet
the romance of history can offer,
they leap off the city walls.
Dangling from driven clouds,
they sail away, singing anthems
as they ascend, never caring
to come down to earth again. [3]

Dale Devereux Barker is a decorative artist in the
best sense – as he luxuriates in the resonances of
language, so also he manipulates the craft
element of his work to seduce the eye. He is not
afraid to make serious gestures through beautiful
things and the best of his public works display a
confidence to use pattern and colour in an
unashamedly dramatic way. The large series of
enamel panels commissioned for St Katharine

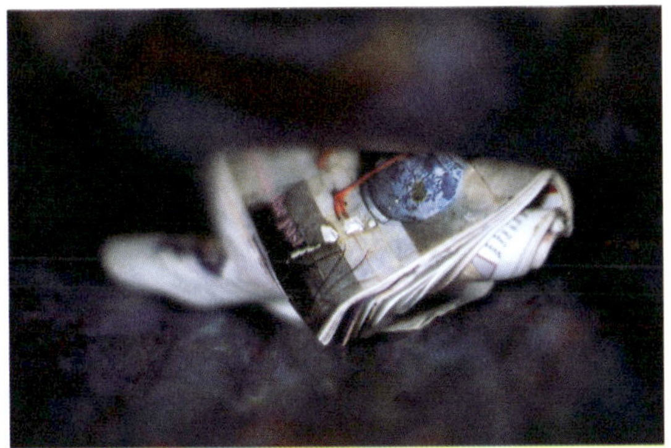

25

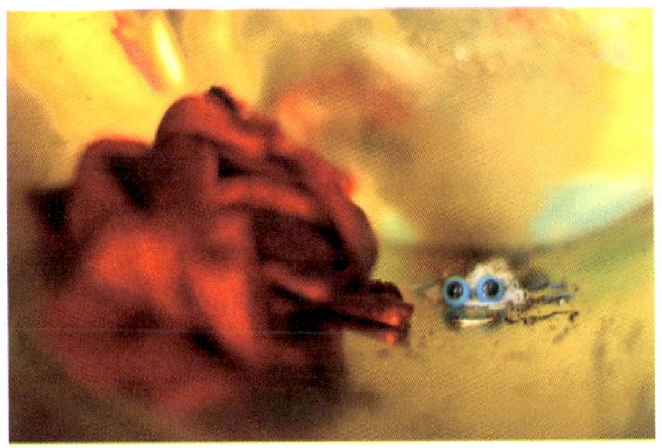

26

Docks was the vibrant response to a potentially unyielding environment of concrete pillars and grey walkways. Translating many of the marks and surfaces from his printmaking, Barker made 135 individual panels, some as isolated still-lives, a great many as repeated pattern, glowing with colour, shimmering in the reflections from the water beneath.

Barker has always made work 'in defence of the pleasure principle' and utilises the particular qualities of each medium to manipulate a response from the viewer. It is somehow fitting that he now stands aside figures such as Bruce McLean or Ian Hamilton Finlay in the collection of Penguin Books. Each is a highly individual artist, working across different disciplines, responding to words, responding to the visual world.

Sixteen Still-Lives

Twenty Titles 1999 takes the work back to the beginning in its simplest form. Looking through it: sixteen reduction lino prints with a letterpress frontispiece; one senses the artist having made this for himself. It is a sequence of images just less than two inches square which show a series of vignettes, mainly of flowers. The printing is a delight – dusky surfaces of silver ink sit lightly over pink and orange backgrounds, a blue veil holds a chaotic composition of objects into place, the lines of a lino take on the refinement of a Japanese print.

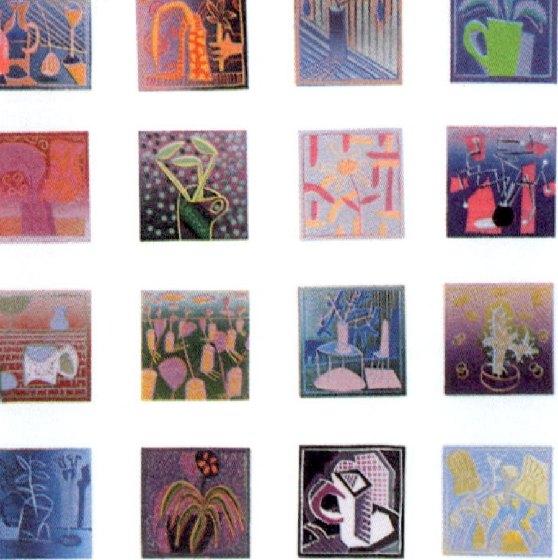

27

notes

1   Emma Hill *The Dreaming Side (no 5)*
    published 1991, The Dinosaur Press/EMH Arts

2   Martin Stannard *From A Recluse to a Roving I Will Go*
    published 1992, The Shed

3   Paul Violi *Under the Boardwalk*
    from *The Hazards of Imagery* published by the artist, 1999

The titles are a wry series of comments on art and on the labour of the artist. The last three are telling:

It's what I'm good at

Arbeit Kunst

It's important

Images

1   Dale Devereux Barker at work, April 1998, Burnham Signs, London. Photographer: Adam Monaghan.

2   Untitled notebook drawing 1997, 150x100mm

3   Untitled notebook drawing 1997, 150x100mm

4   **Confused** 1992, vitreous enamel 1685x1685mm commissioned by Clifford Chance, London. Photographer: Simon Marsh

5   **Time takes time** 1992, vitreous enamel 1685x1685mm commissioned by Clifford Chance, London. Photographer: Simon Marsh

6   **Artists, models and decorative devices** 1994, mixed media on paper 710mmx510mm, private collection

7   **Empire of the senses** 1989, silkscreen print, 765x570mm, edition of 10, private collections

8   **Bohemian Girl** 1997, mixed media collage on paper 350x350mm, corporate collection, London

9   **Variations on the human form** 1982, drawings 150x100mm each, whereabouts unknown

10   From **The Living Set** 1986, reduction linocut 127x127mm

11   **All good things they say never last**, from **The Living Set** 1986, reduction linocut, 127x127mm, private collections

12   **Diary of a Has-been** 1995, reduction linocut 250x250mm, edition of 12, private collections

13   **Swum** 1989, reduction linocut 150x150mm, edition of 8

14   **Technique** 1999, reduction linocut 300x300mm, edition of 3

15   **The Water's Fine** 1991, reduction linocut 152x201mm, edition of 20, private collections

16   **Here I am** 1991, reduction linocut 152x201mm, edition of 20

17   **Very Quick Indeed** 1990, reduction linocut 152x201mm, edition of 20

18   **Big Love** 1990, reduction linocut 152x201mm, edition of 20, private collections

19   **Physically, Mentally, Emotionally** 1990, reduction linocut 152x201mm, edition of 20, private collections

20   **Pursuit** 1990, reduction linocut 152x201mm, edition of 20

21   Installation **The Hazards of Imagery**, The Eagle Gallery, London 1999

22   Linocut from **The Dreaming Side**, published by The Dinosaur Press, London 1991

23   Drawing from **A Recluse to a Roving I Will Go** published by The Shed, Ipswich, 1992

24   Drawing from **A Recluse to a Roving I Will Go** published by The Shed, Ipswich, 1992

25   From a series of photographs taken by Roderick Packe at the artist's home and studio, 4–6 December 1999

26   From a series of photographs taken by Roderick Packe at the artist's home and studio, 4–6 December 1999

27   **Twenty Titles** 1999, reduction linocut, 16 blocks each 60x60mm printed on a single sheet, edition of 10. Also published by The Black Shed, Capel St. Mary, Ipswich, as a boxed set of single plates, edition of 16

28   Untitled, silkscreen ink on layered sheets of perspex, 28 works each 600x460x50mm, commissioned by Penguin Books, London, May 1998

29   Untitled collage 1998, 255x355mm

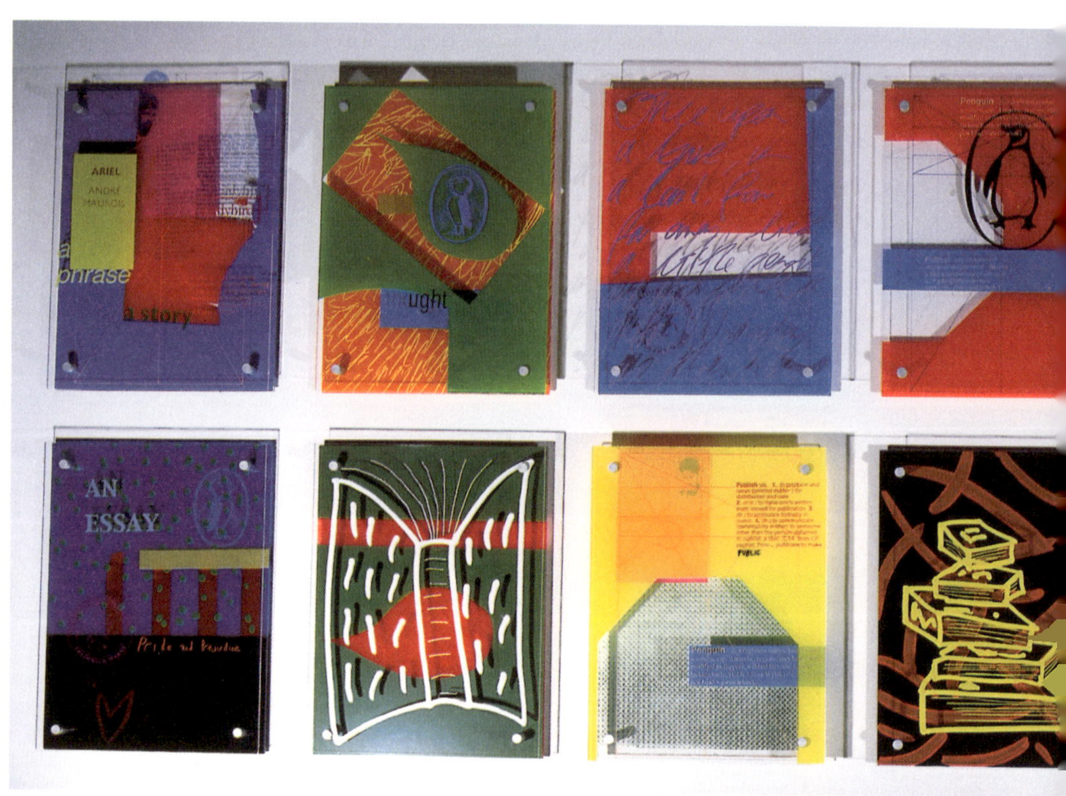

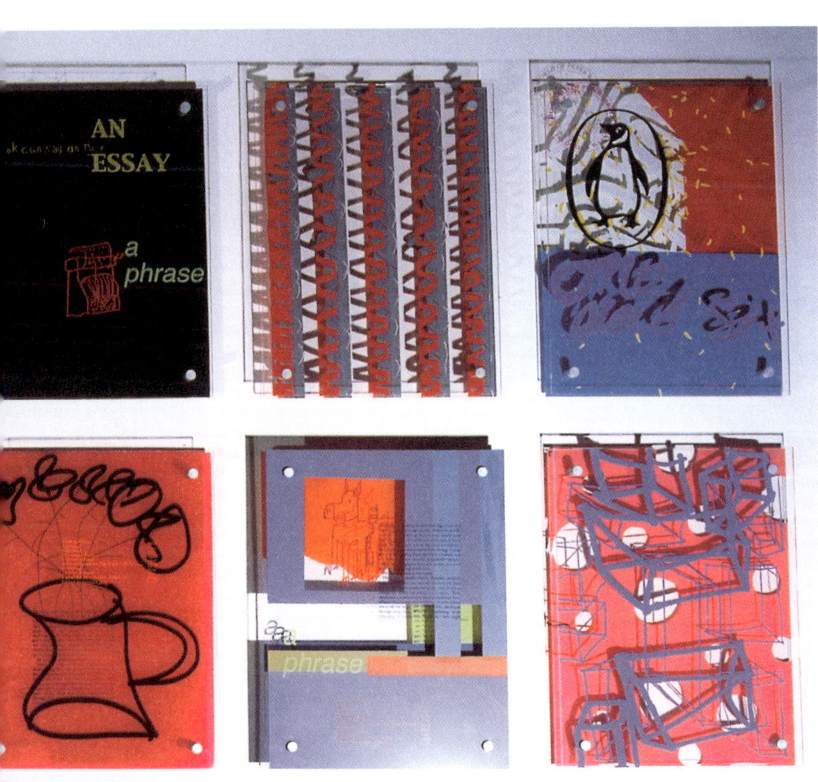
AN
ESSAY
a
phrase

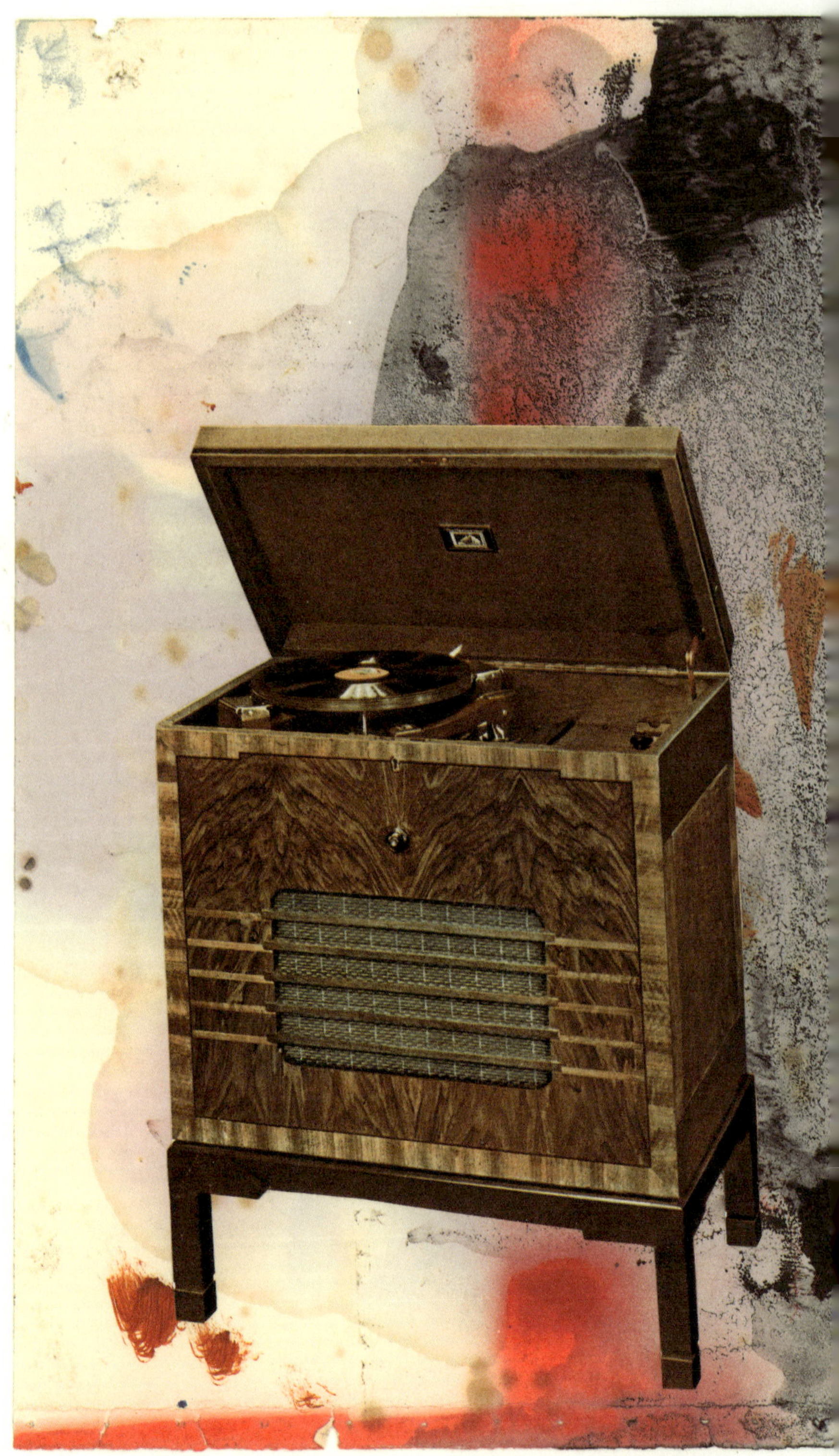

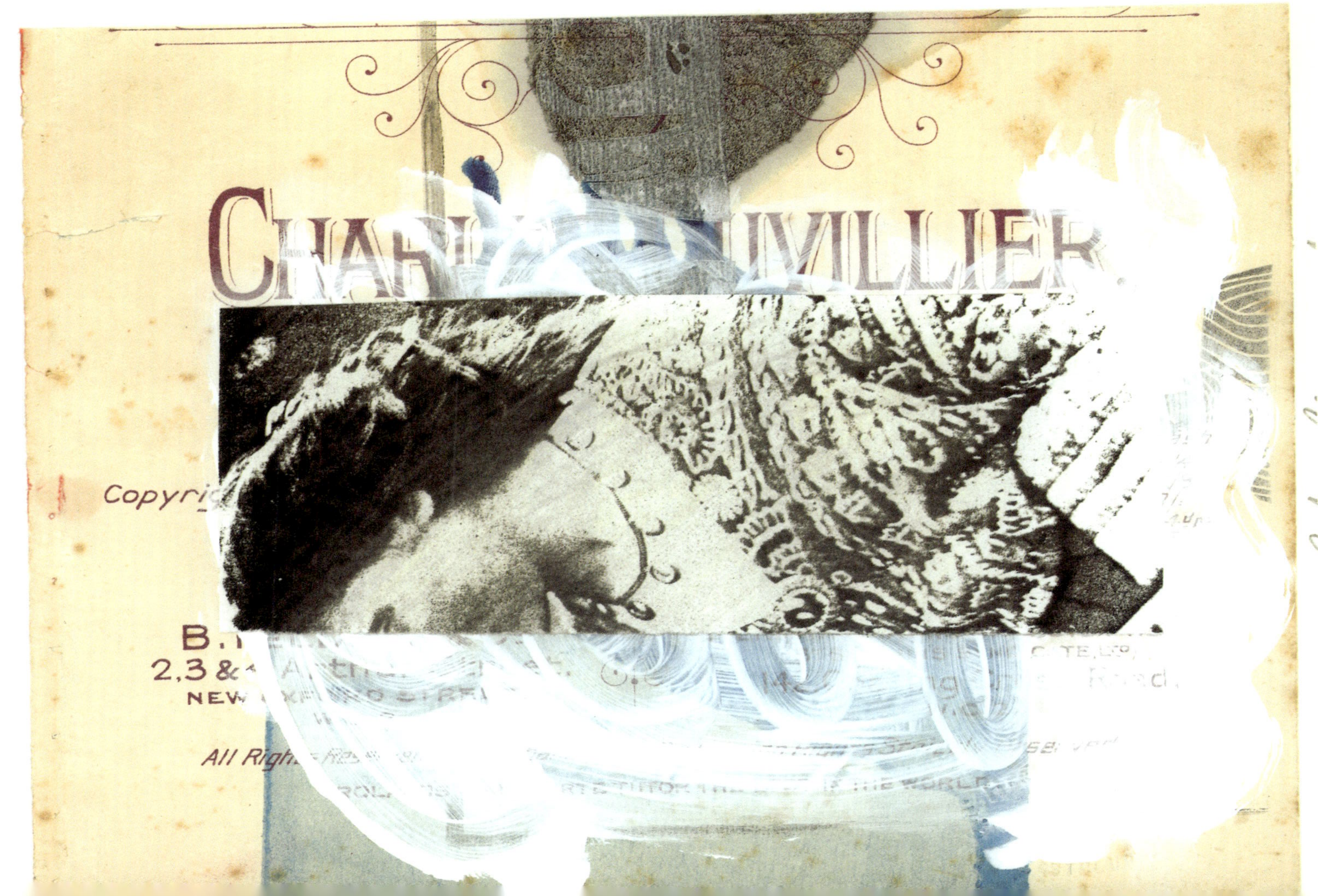

CHAPPELL DUVILLIER
Copyrig
B.
2,3 &
NEW
All Rights

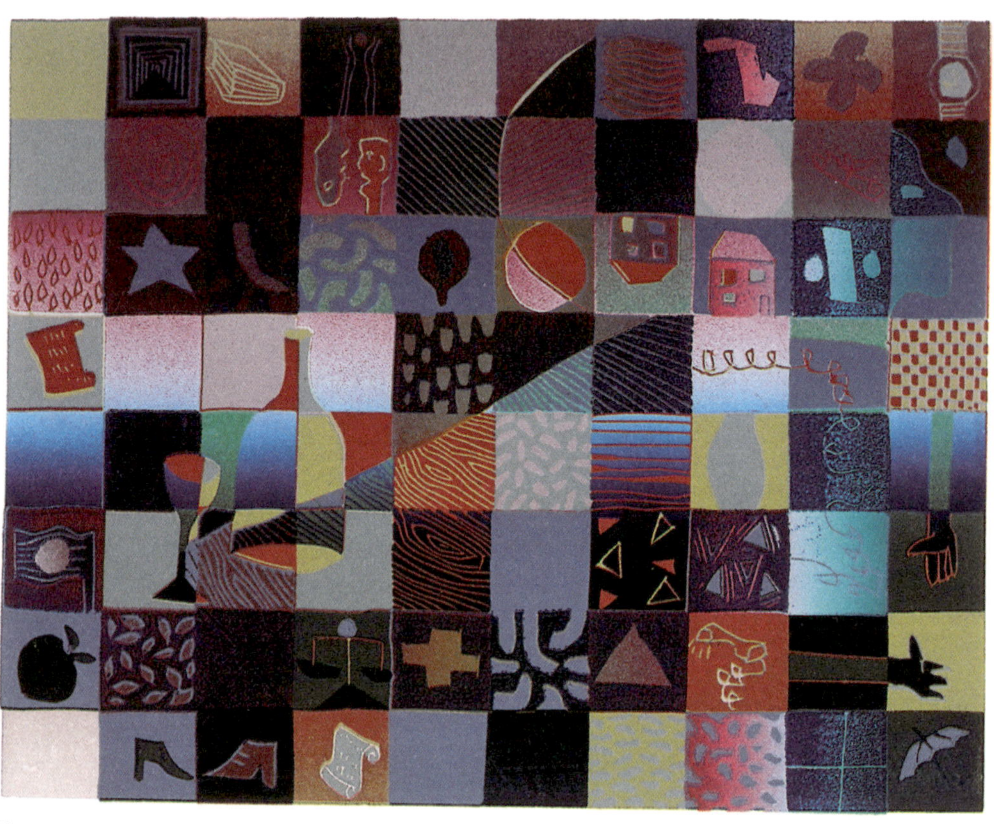

30

Shopping List

Steve Hoskins

I was approached to write this text through a letter from Dale Devereux Barker. Whilst honoured to be asked to write about this artist and printmaker, whose career I have followed with much interest; the factor which most influenced my agreeing was a sentence which said. 'Whilst a big proportion of the show will be print-generated, the last thing I'm trying to do is another old procession of techno self-indulgence. Essentially it's a show about the joys of making. It just so happens that print is one of the most exciting ways to make something.' Why then, is print so exciting at this point in time?

It is over a thousand years to the traceable origins of print in China and Korea, and five hundred years since the birth of modern printing and the development of movable type in western Europe. Fundamentally, many of the elements of those early processes have not changed to this day. If one views a Dürer woodblock or a Plantin Bible, from the purely technical standpoint they are impossible to date accurately. This time-line has continued unbroken well into the twentieth century and only now at the end of the millennium is that continuing tradition being questioned and perhaps fundamentally challenged.

Within the modern graphic artist's armoury, that line remains unbroken. Relief printing is rooted in the fifteenth century, with little change in process or technique from the work of Dürer. The roots of etching are in the seventeenth century, with the work of Seeghers and Rembrandt. Today we still use recipes for grounds and varnishes developed in that period. Lithography stems from the eighteenth century with Senefelder; many printers still swear by the unsurpassed flexibility

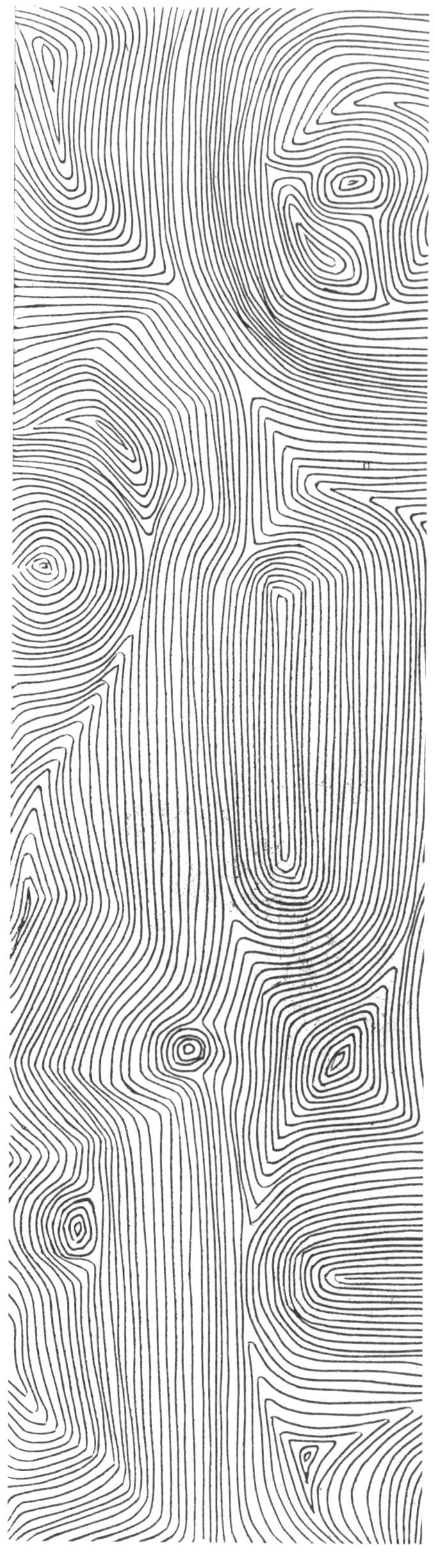

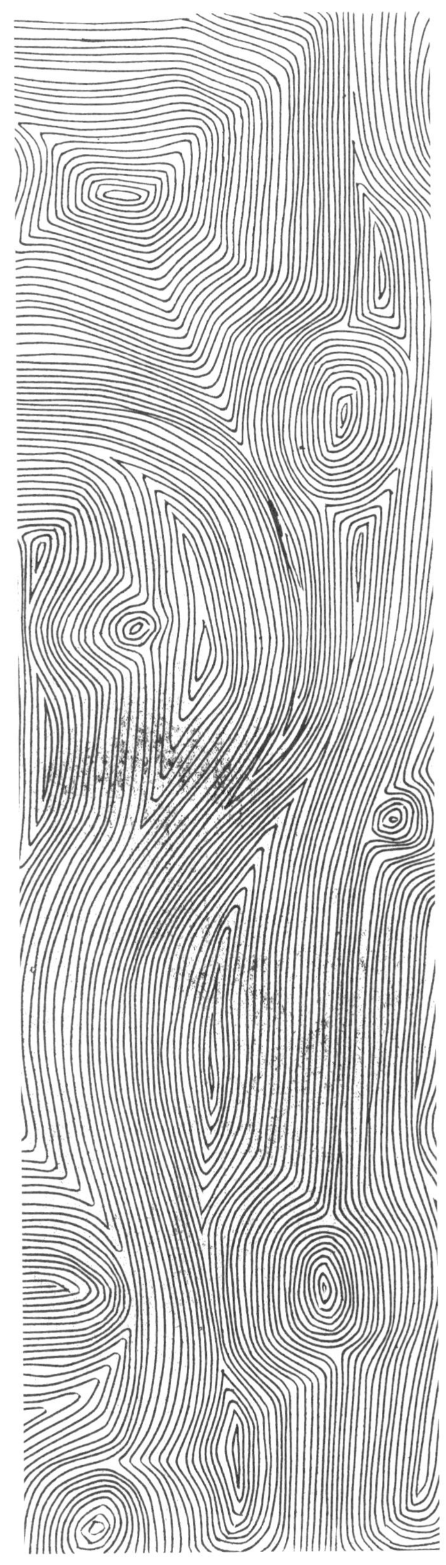

of working on limestone. Photography dates from the nineteenth with Fox Talbot and Karl Klic, both of whose contributions to photogravure have been reassessed in the last two decades. Screenprinting is the twentieth century print process, most influenced by Warhol in the USA and Chris Prater in Europe. Now into the arena enters digital media, increasingly seen and accepted as perhaps the most powerful visual tool since printed imagery came into existence. A fundamental question is whether the debate about the death of print is conditioned by the advent of digital technology, or is the collective consciousness at the end of the twentieth century driving the appraisal, with the digital as merely a catalyst?

As a medium printmaking has two fascinating attributes. Firstly it has the ability to produce multiple images and, at its best, this makes it the most democratic of artforms. Images can be produced cheaply and through visual expression, have the power to attempt to influence society, even induce change. In a recent introduction to a portfolio of prints celebrating South Africa's Bill of Human Rights, The most Reverend Desmond Tutu said 'The images powerfully complement the words of the bill of rights. Given our history, they serve as an apt reminder that words, however inspiring and lyrical, have been used as much to subvert as to create. It is therefore necessary to portray our commitment to human rights in pictures, which are less open to corruption.'

Secondly, there is the process of collaboration. It is not possible to be a printmaker and never have to deal with other people. To even begin making a print one either has to be taught by another or work at a collaborative studio which will produce the print for you. Making a print is then both a decisive and discursive activity.

It is possible at this juncture to take two views as to the future of printmaking. One is that as a medium of expression, in the dying embers of the twentieth century, printmaking is an outdated and outmoded force only perpetuated by people who hide behind the mystique of old technical process to the detriment of an original idea or concept. Having hung around on the coat-tails of painting for hundreds of years, it has been finally killed off in the last century by the advent of the moving image. It has become the screen based culture of the new millennium, accessible from any point in the world at the touch of a computer keyboard.

The other view is that printmaking has a long future. Being essentially a collaborative, communal process, one that shifts its outlook and perceptions, encompassing the new without at the same time discarding the old. Founded for its best practitioners on a deep rooted love of surface quality and craft that by definition, goes beyond the desire to just shock or gain a quick reaction. Printmaking deals with visual qualities and elegance that comes only from experience and knowledge. Dale Devereux Barker himself has said 'There is an approach that places the importance of the image beyond the method of making and as such, welcomes any aid to achieving the desired result.'

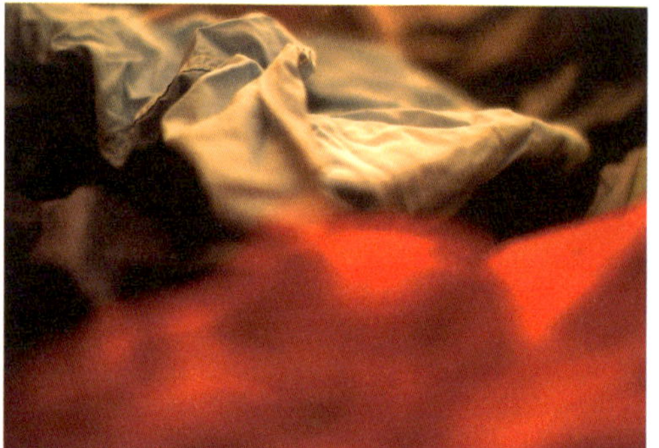

31

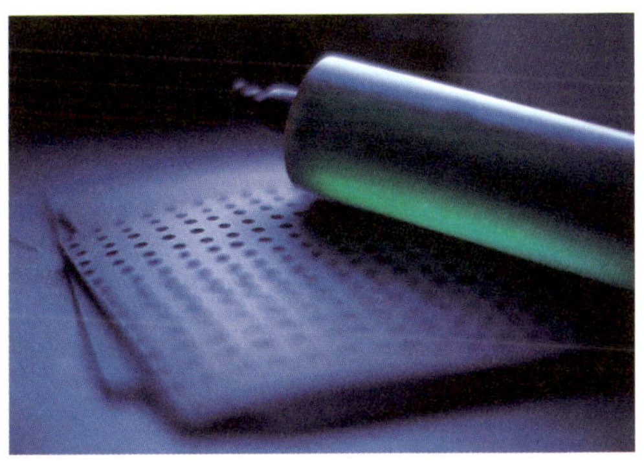

32

This begs the question 'Why printmaking?' Ask any printmaker and you get one of three answers. Primarily there is a quality of surface and tactility sustained from handling a sheet of paper (taken in this context to include other printed substrates) and a means of control of surface and colour offered by no other visual medium. The element of touch and feel is very important to printmakers. It allows an intimacy with small elements, which can have major influences on the final quality and outcome. This naturally leads to a greater emphasis on how those qualities are conveyed and, if they are not present, the conveying of content will always suffer. Therefore an interest in the technical 'nuts and bolts' of print creation is essential to good printmaking. This creates the late twentieth century printmaker's dilemma. You cannot be a good printmaker without knowledge of technical process, yet in acknowledging technique you lay yourself open to criticism that technique overrides content. It is a well-known fact that if you put two printmakers in a room with a print the first question they will ask is 'How's it done?' This is not invariably a denial of content, merely a common ground attempt to form the necessary collaborative dialogue that is essential to function as a printmaker. Finally, therefore, it is that very process of collaboration that printmakers will also cite as integral to the practice of the discipline. It is in the collaborative studios of the last fifty years that some of the best and most innovative work has been created.

Where then does this place printmaking today? Before putting contemporary print practice in context, one has to look at the influence of digital technology on the discipline. What constitutes the term 'digital' in this context? For the sake of argument, digitisation here means physical output from the computer in a tangible form, ie printed.

The means of output are either as inkjet or iris prints directly printed from computer onto a substrate, usually paper, that is a direct result of scanning and manipulation on the computer. Or digitisation is seen as a means of gathering material to be used and converting that material to a form that is directly usable within the traditional print process framework. An example of this is a small drawing or found object, scanned straight to computer with little or no manipulation, and then output in the form of photo quality negative or positive to be directly made into a screenprint or lithographic stencil. These two methods of using the digital are commonplace. However it is a third reaction to, rather than method of use of, digitisation which is the most interesting.

With the adoption of digitisation by industry as cost benefits drive rapid change, the commercial need for some print processes has disappeared. This cost benefit analysis has been a fact of life for the last five hundred years. Computer typesetting heralded the demise of traditional handset type as early as the 1970s. Now that these processes are taken for granted, a further evolution is in process. Artists are reappraising the old processes, not for the sake of resurrecting an old craft skill, but rather posing the question; 'Is there a quality of function or aesthetic that has been lost and/or is there a possibility of a different outcome if this old process is married to new technology?'

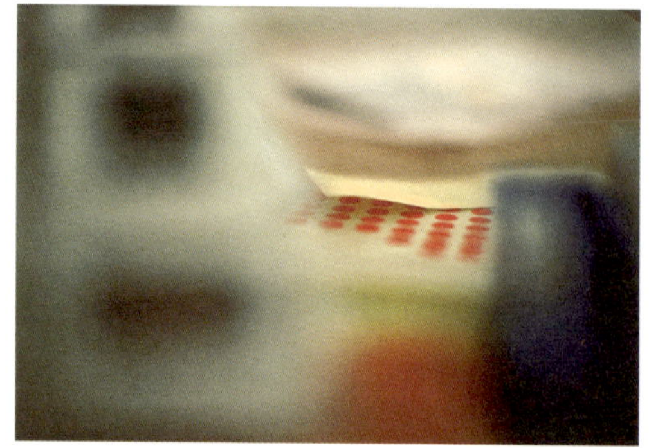

33

Two examples of this marriage would be the re-introduction of handset metal type and of process photography. Within typography computer setting is ubiquitous. Yet the most popular course we run, at the University of the West of England Print Centre, is typesetting by hand. The reason is that, although typesetting by computer is totally dominant, the terminology has not changed. The easiest way to learn the function of leading, type height, kerning and upper and lower cases, is to set type physically. Once learnt never forgotten, and the job of typesetting by computer becomes consequently much smoother.

The outcome of these changes is less straightforward. Computer setting enabled artists and writers to publish small numbers of copies very cheaply and quickly. This in turn led to a boom in the Artists Book as a contemporary artform. This boom has been sustained and further fuelled by the new generations' interest in typesetting because of qualities unobtainable elsewhere. Yet it is also possible to say the Artists Book is a direct reaction to digital technology and a return to the hand crafted statement.

Process photography is the other example. Currently digital photography and programmes such as Photoshop, have driven wet process darkrooms almost to the point of extinction. Whereas ten years ago a photographer and his assistants would carefully set up and light the background to a shot, then the printer would lovingly hand dodge the background to the art director's requirements. Now the Photoshop operator scans in the necessary, adds a few layers and makes a couple of adjustments from Kai's power tools. Time taken: 20 minutes. Fine art

34

photographers are now looking back at what has
gone before in the same way as typographers.
Embracing the digital but asking what has been
lost, some of the answer appears to lie in old
photomechanical processes, such as
photogravure and platinum printing. These
archival processes enable the finest quality digital
output to be enhanced and preserved. Allowing
the new whilst retaining the flexibility and
delicacy of the old craft skills.

What does this have to do with contemporary
printmaking practice ? The answer is a choice. All
of these areas and debates are up for grabs and
open for exploration. Never before has such a
diverse range of opportunities been open to the
artist formerly known as a printmaker. The best of
the current practitioners are making the most of
this new territory and are exploring the
boundaries.

However, it is not possible to conduct such an
exploration without having a base from which to
work. It is in such a context that artists such as
Dale Devereux Barker play a key role in
contemporary printmaking practice. Rooted firmly
in the history of print, Dale Devereux Barker's
base is one of the simplest forms, the reduction
linocut. This is not a constraint – Dale has learnt to
deal with and revel in all the formal traditions of
printmaking. He has a sensibility for colour and
form that has developed over the years in which
he has become familiar with the medium. The
content is now available to be read by the viewer.
At the same time the understanding and joy of the
process allows a further seamless dialogue
between the content, the viewer and the means
by which it is presented.

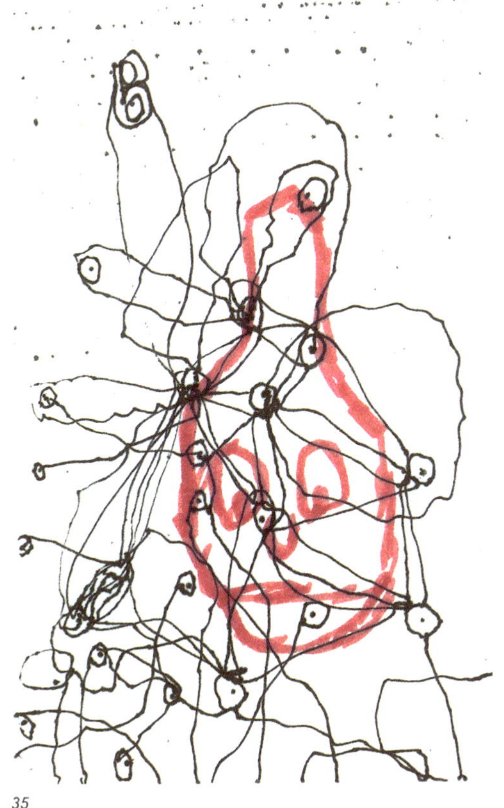

The content, in harmony with the method of presentation, is presented in clear pared down fragments, drawn from everyday life. The juxtaposition of those fragments presents a narrative that relates both to the way we receive visual information and to recent printmaking history.

This firm ground has given him the confidence and excitement to explore parallel territory. He has recently ventured into another of those areas contemporary printmaking is exploring – printed enamel on metal. Recent commissions have allowed a collaboration with *Burnham Signs*, the industrial producers of enamel on metal panels for architectural use. This work brings print into the area of permanent public art and the function negates the normal mode of multiple replication. Yet the modes of working are identical to the core methods which root his work within the field.

Other means of using a combination of hand rendered (autographic) and pre-defined images are evident in such work as the Penguin Books commission. The narrative runs through a series of hand rendered images connected by a pre-defined and familiar set of Penguin icons from the publisher, interspersed with text. There are close parallels with 1960s iconography, even to the use of perspex panels to print upon, yet the means of reproduction are contemporary. What Dale Devereux Barker reflects is an increasing use of found and digital imagery used through a third party process. When combined with a high degree of craft skills, these create a highly sophisticated and visually appealing artwork.

When assessing work of this nature, one
overriding fact is apparent, that of an artist who
enjoys making work. The excitement of creating
art, combined with a love of making and a desire
to make work that has a visual elegance – these
are concepts which do not have to be missing
in order to make art that is relevant to
contemporary issues.

This is a culture that has been much neglected in
the last decade. Hopefully, the acceptance that
art is poorer without the joy of making will
become a mainstream attitude once again in the
next century.

Images

30   **Hints and Tips** 1991, reduction linocut 200x250mm,
     edition of 20

31–33   From a series of photographs taken by Roderick Packe
     at the artist's home and studio, 4–6 December 1999

34   From **The Luddite Series** 1996, reduction linocut
     215x180mm, unique

35   Untitled notebook drawing 1997, 150x100mm

36   **Still Life II** 1992, reduction linocut 240x180mm,
     edition of 20

37   Untitled 1998, vitreous enamel 3.8x45 metres,
     commissioned by Taylor-Woodrow Properties plc and
     The Pool of London Partnership, St Katharine Docks,
     London. Photographer: Simon Marsh

38   Detail of above

39   Detail of above

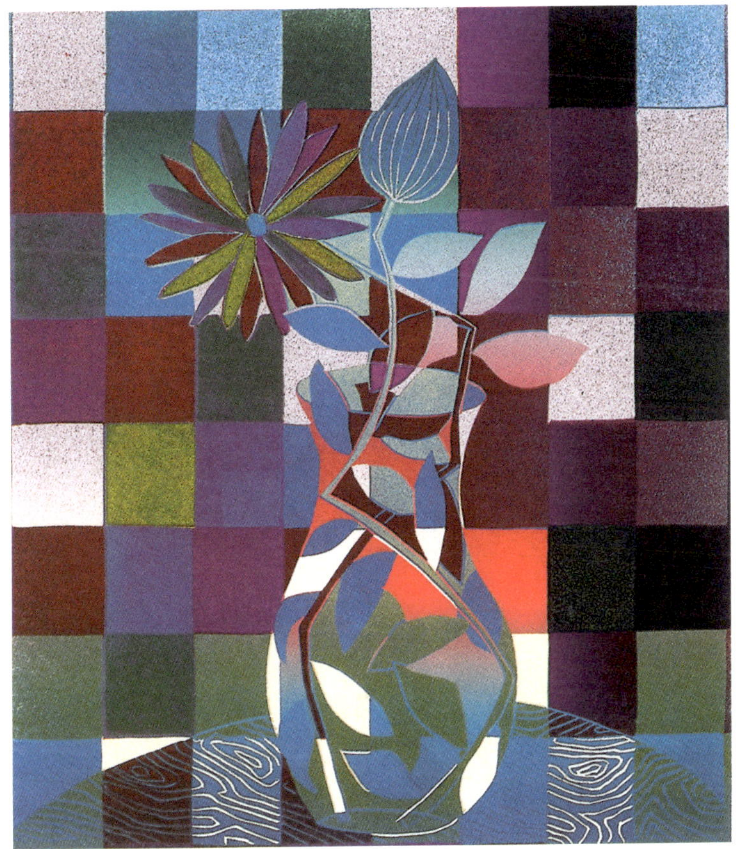

36

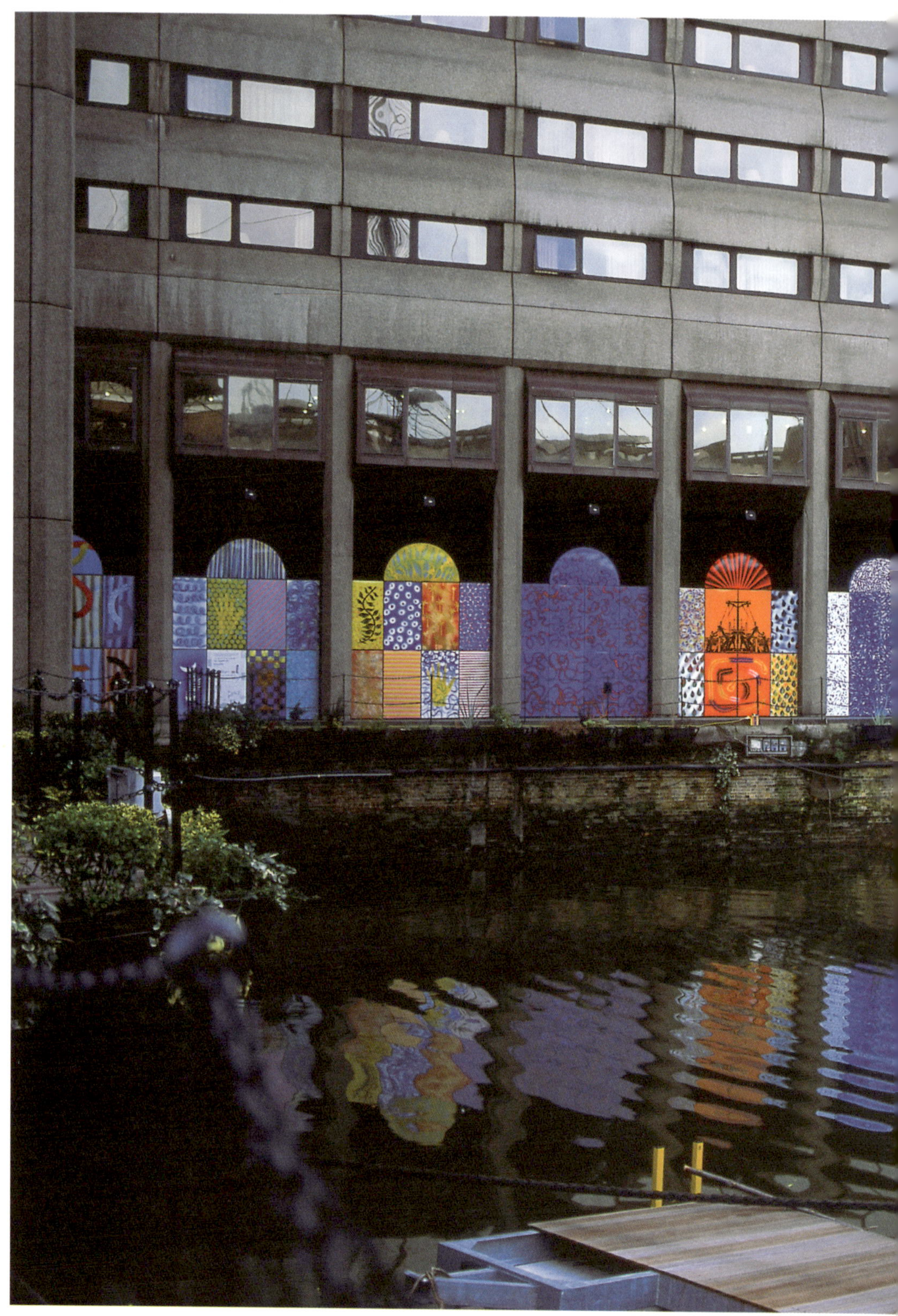

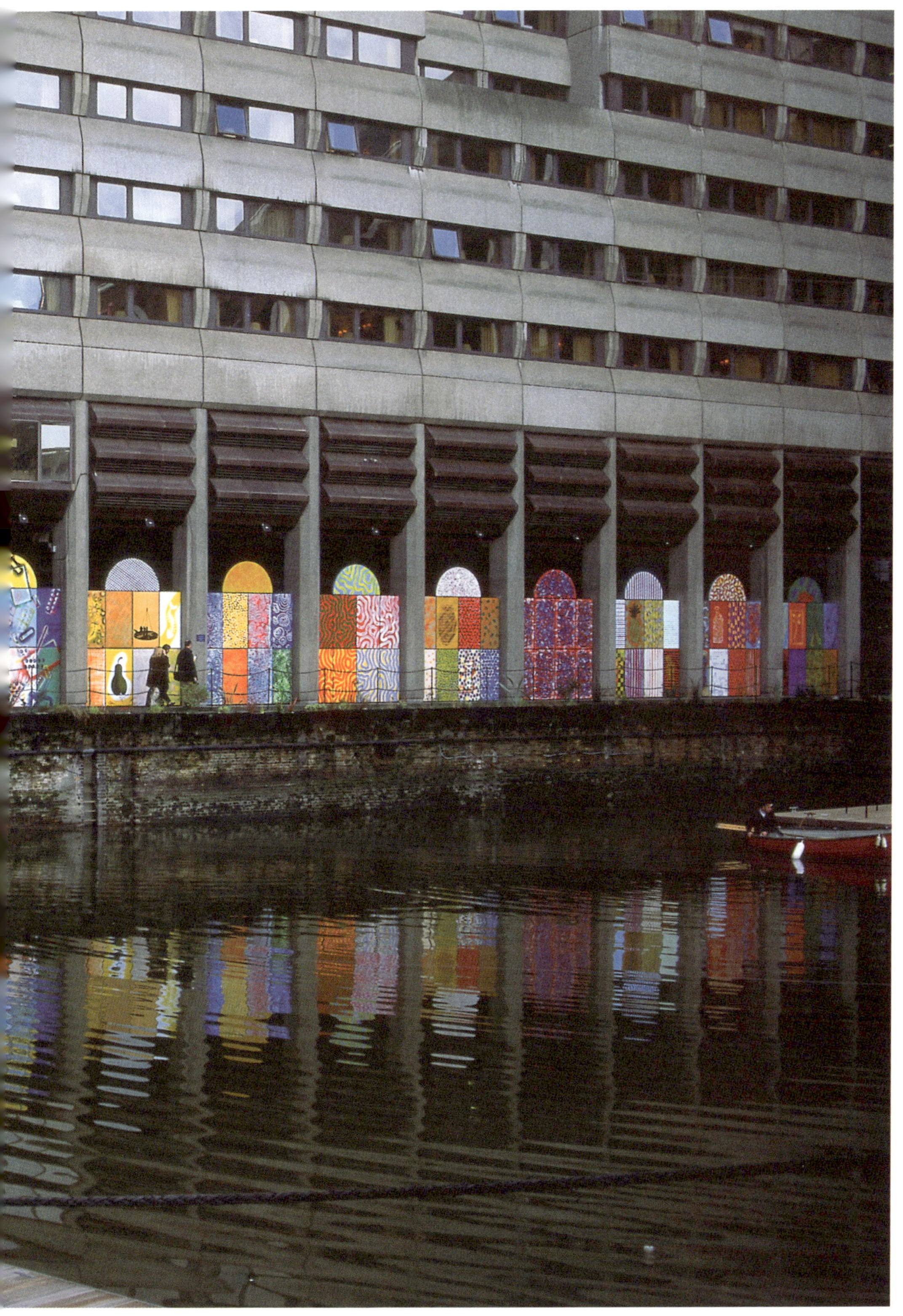

38

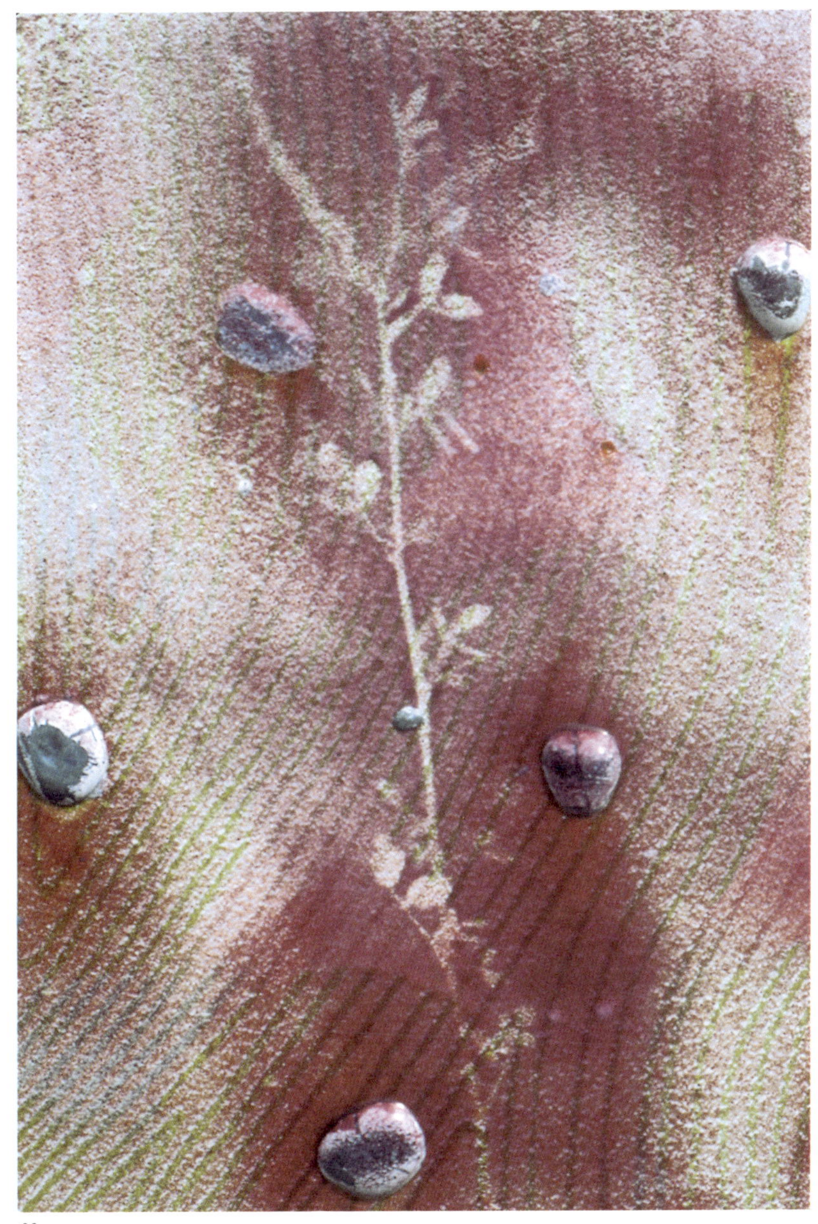

39

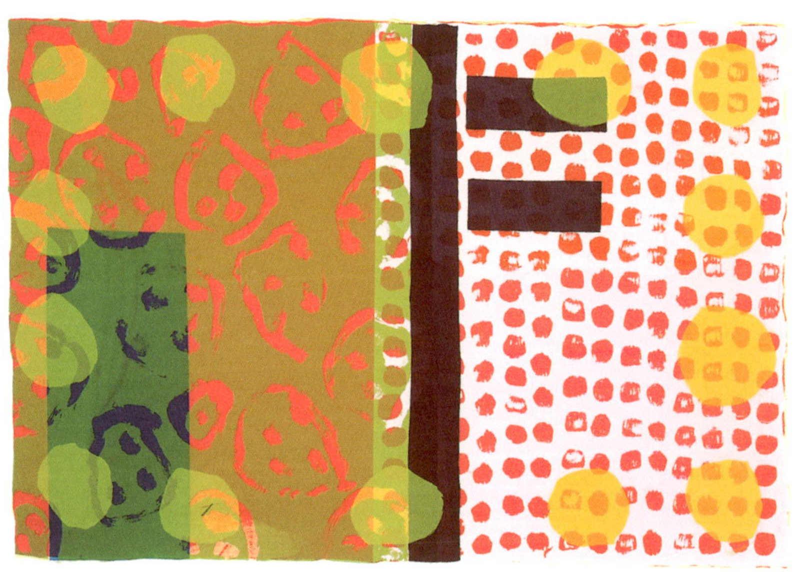

40

Making Art

Adam Monaghan

Art and craft share an unquestionably peculiar relationship. Since the Renaissance and the emergence of the cult of the artist as hero and genius, a divide has existed which has both created and imposed cultural and interpretive hierarchies. The divide traditionally positions art at the top and leaves craft to loiter somewhere below: fine art, so the story goes, holds more aesthetic value and is better equipped for serious intellectual questioning – both from the artist and its audience. But, in more recent times interesting problems have arisen with this relationship and called into question many of the academic and social assumptions that we have previously made.

For over 400 years, craft or rather craftsmanship, had largely been the guiding light for the appreciation of art. Works were admired for their technical expertise, their detail, their likeness and ultimately, for their demonstration of a skill the audience did not share. Thus the artist's elevated position perpetually fuelled itself so long as the artist produced works of art which could be defined in craft terms. The advent of abstraction dramatically altered these perceptions. The concept that the artist did not have to visually demonstrate a craft talent was perhaps furthered most significantly by Marcel Duchamp. Duchamp declared that it was not important that the artist had even made the work with his own hand, but rather that he had chosen it.

Over the course of this century, since Marcel Duchamp first explored the notion of the 'ready-made', the artist as maker has slipped in and out of favour. However, in more recent history, and notably since Warhol and Pop Art, the equation has been complicated and intellectualised by a multitude of academic and artistic theories. Where

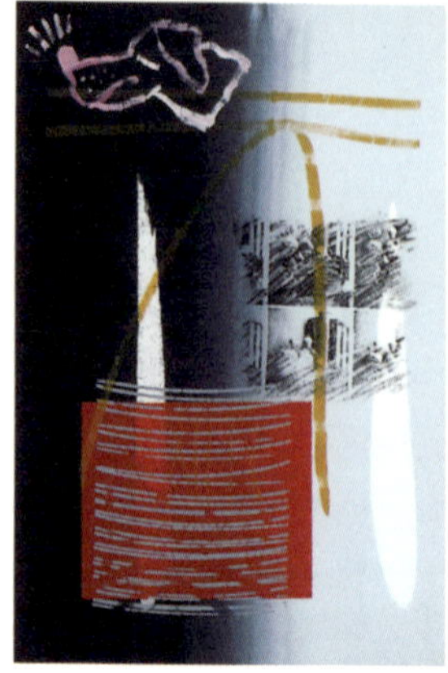

41

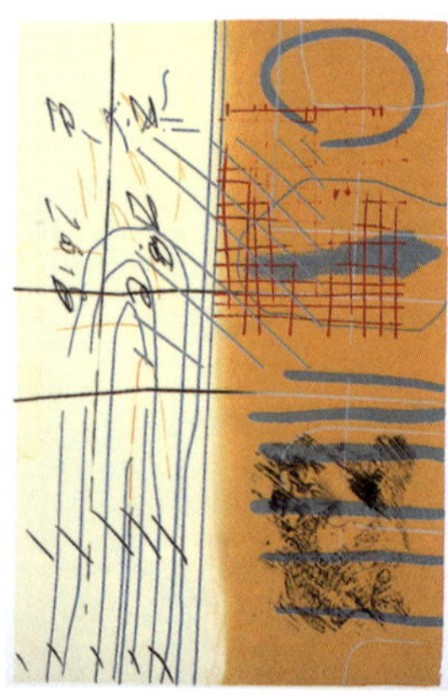

42

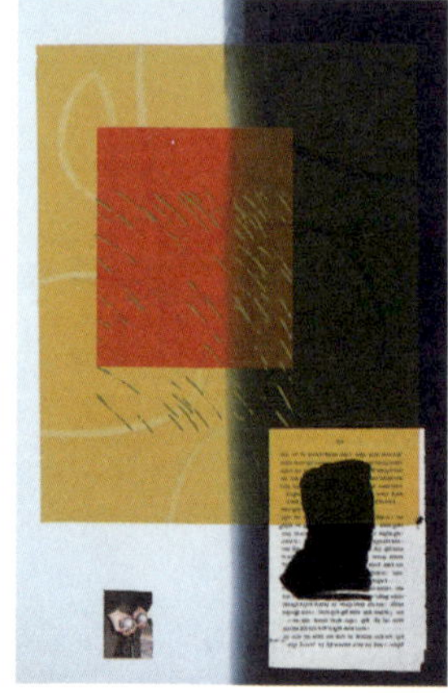

43

virtuosity and representation had been replaced with true expression of the self in pure colour, form and composition, postmodernity presented the impression of such true expression. What you saw was no longer what you got. There would no longer be a definitive line between left and right, black and white or right and wrong. Everything was potentially something else. Ironic, kitsch or actual were becoming increasingly inseparable.

Postmodernism has reintroduced the appropriation of other people's skills. If, as Duchampian theory had declared, art was in the idea and not its execution, then artists are free to employ other people's talents. If artists wanted to produce an end product rather than demonstrate a particular individual 'making' skill then why not simply employ another person to make it? In doing this, the artist can avoid the final art work's interpretation being hampered by technical difficulties or manufacturing amateurism. Such ways of working mean that the artist is freer to move from medium to medium, choosing whatever instrument is most suitable for their end product. Indeed the execution may intentionally have nothing to do with the art work's aim and any dialogue with craft or manufacture may only be raised by its glaring omission.

It is within such grey areas that Dale Devereux Barker explores some interesting quandaries. Here is an artist who is serious about the production of his work and acutely aware of the art history that he is indebted to, but is not confined by either environment. Whilst it is important that the works are made, it is never totally engulfed by the making process; they always remain works of art that are framed by art world references and intellectual and visual juxtaposition.

Although he has long been labelled a printmaker, Dale Devereux Barker has always explored a variety of media. Indeed, Barker was trained as a painter and he still regards his printing as a process which is more informed by painting than traditional printmaking. So why is it that with such a painterly background, print has formed such a substantial part of Barker's work? What is it about print that is so special?

Historically printmaking has been a process whereby images were made cheaply available to a wider market and so print has remained with a different value system to painting. Hence today, it is part of a middle ground that is neither craft or directly part of the canon. Indeed many artists working in print use it as an additional medium to their main practice. (It is worth considering how important Picasso's prints would have been without the significance of his painting)? Print has thus never truly been the recognised medium of 'great art.' However, there are advantages to this situation. The tradition and heroism of painting is capable of overawing many potential projects; the blank canvas and loaded brush can be deeply inhibiting materials. In contrast, those processes traditionally seen as craft, (print, ceramic and enamelling), have much less daunting histories and as such can be played with and pushed about to a greater degree. In the case of print, this is, of course, helped by the nature of the process which depressurises the individual work and thus may act as a medium which liberates the production of further work.

Like many craft techniques print also places a process between the artist's hand and the final product. Whether screen, roller, block or acid, methods of printing impose a procedure that the

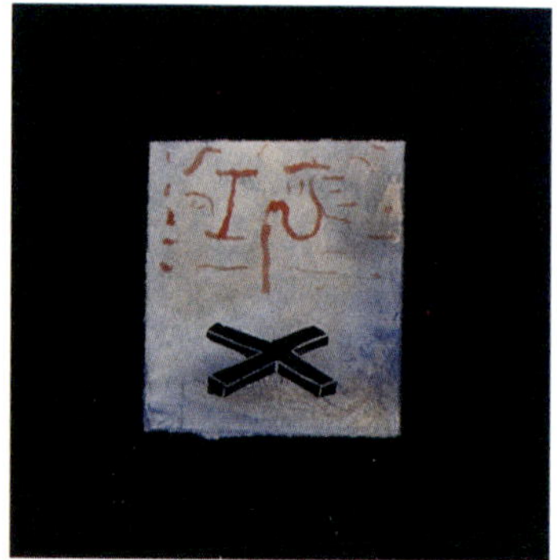

44

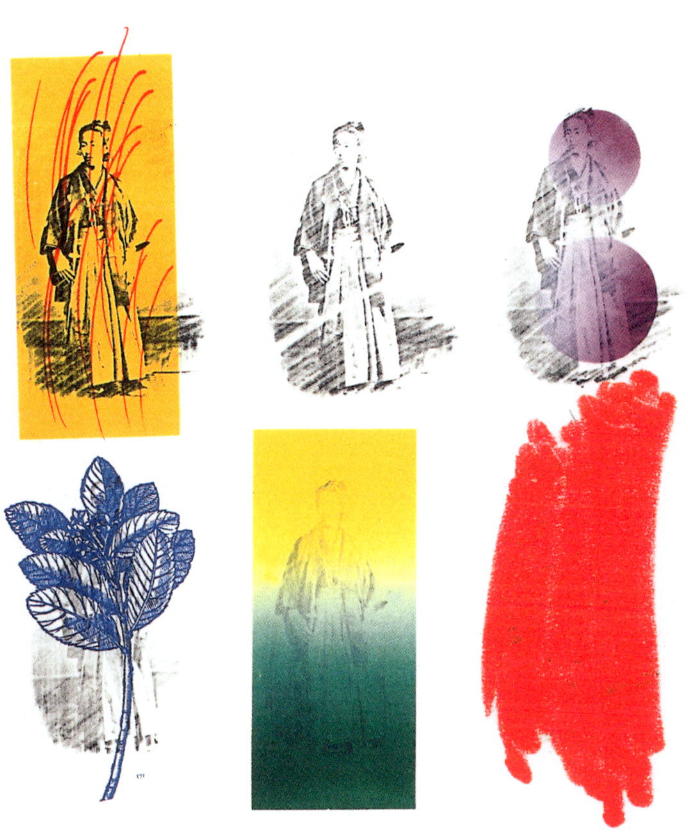

45

artist has to confront. Such a process is inherently
labour intensive and well suited to Barker's
extraordinary work ethic – a quality he both
attributes to and blames on a working class
background. It is ironic to note that much of Barker's
work follows this theme – hands on and yet never
totally touched. Print, enamelling and ceramics all
remove the artist from direct control of the work at
some point in its production. There is always an
element of something else happening to the work.
Once again, this notion of serendipity is something
that is deliberately played to. Barker experiments
with the formal processes of production and
remains excited by the potential of these trials on
subsequent work. Making fortuitous experiments is
an exercise that is often undervalued, indeed it
betrays the very nature of the hard won image. But
the unexpected is important and it brings with it a
light hearted, accessible side to the work. After all,
one can be as serious about celebrating life as one
is condemning it.

However, this does not mean that Barker has rested
on his laurels. More recently the ethic of print has
been extended into vast public art works. In a
commission for Taylor-Woodrow and The Pool of
London Partnership at St. Katharine Docks, Barker
made one hundred and thirty five 160x80cm
vitreous enamel panels which now form the
backdrop to the East side of the dock. The work
both demonstrates Barker's ability to work on a
huge scale and reiterates his commitment to making
his works. Unlike many artists who make work at
the end of a 'phone line, Barker spent five months
in the factory. Whilst he is quite comfortable
working away from his own studio, the intensity of
the factory brought with it different considerations
from those the artist is usually forced to make.

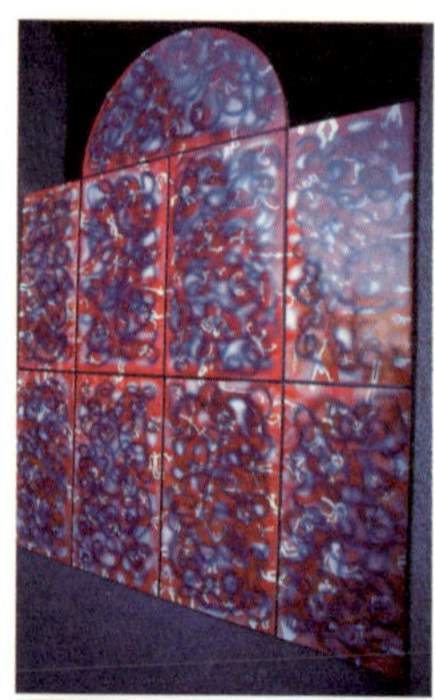

46

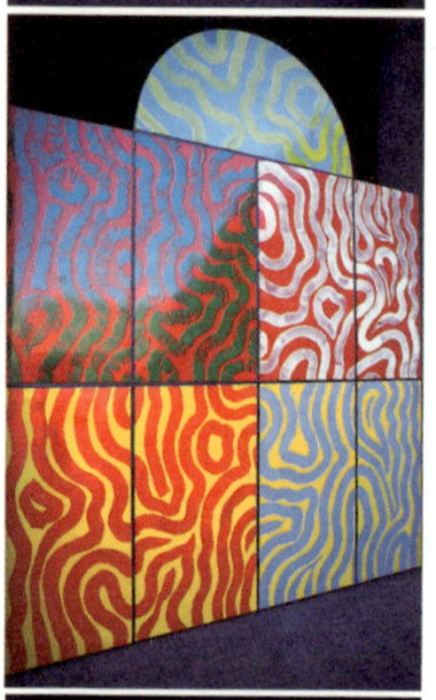

47

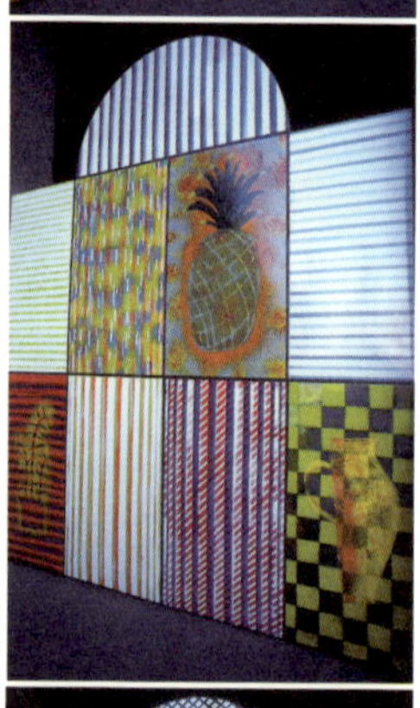

48

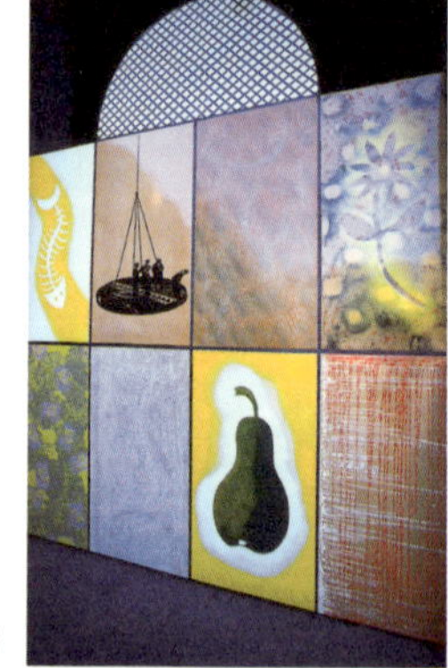

49

Whilst the gap between intimate linocuts and gigantic public enamels may seem considerable, there are specific likenesses between the printing and enamelling processes. Like print, enamelling relies on areas of the work's production being outside the artist's immediate control. There are inescapable parallels between peeling away the paper, lifting the screen and winching away the kiln door. There is also a similarity in the application of colour and in its eventual tactile qualities. Once again, the similarities in process and the working intensity seem altogether in line with Barker's ethic of making. But nevertheless, enamelling is a markedly less accessible process for the maker than it is for the viewer – the practice requires specialist materials and substantial equipment rarely seen in the artist's studio.

It is interesting to see that more recently Barker has again begun to exhibit painting. Whilst it is possible that the successes of other recent work has rejuvenated his confidence and laid to rest some earlier personal frustrations, Barker also acknowledges that after the sheer scale and production procedure of enamelling, it was important for him to return to a more intimate medium. Where the printed word or image is often culturally interpreted as equating to 'fact', paint can be seen to be more personal, more ambiguous and more fluid. This again highlights the irony of the two mediums' relationship; both are ultimately as free and independent as the other, but within their own specific histories. Barker is thus cautious of reinforcing painting's hierarchical position above print and some recent paintings intriguingly have a peculiar 'print' feel to them. Ultimately, it is as though the ethic of each medium has been addressed through the

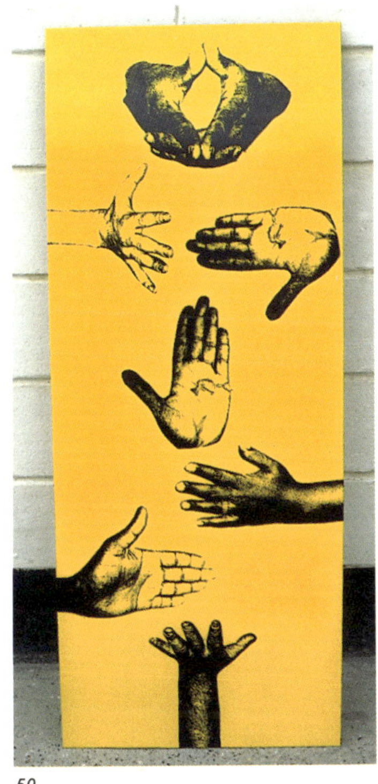

50

language, and with knowledge of the other. This gives Barker's paintings the benefit of a similar quirky, light-hearted feel to his prints – a notion that is often strongly reinforced by his offbeat subject matter.

Perhaps the appeal of Dale Devereux Barker's work initially lies in this very accessibility and variation. For although Barker is a renowned printmaker, a wider survey of his work displays the true depth of his abilities. It also quickly becomes apparent how paradoxical Barker's work can be. Print sometimes looks like paint, paint like print; the work is serious and yet amusing, contemporary but still aesthetic, hand crafted but manufactured, and unique works are made through mass production techniques. Such paradoxes are, of course, inherently humorous; the unexpected, the contradictory, the ironic are all capable of producing a wry, knowing smile. With Barker's work the smile often lingers as interpretation winds its way through the image's potential possibilities and inevitably back to Barker himself. With him there is always a reassuring belief that the more traditional qualities of artistic production are still intact; a sense of history, craftsmanship, work ethic, honesty and a respect and understanding of materials. But there is also something else: a freshness to the approach of such traditions, an openness and curiosity and unfailing energy that can only come from a thorough understanding of the workings of our contemporary environment.

Images

40   **Murphy's Law** 1992, silkcreen 460x660mm, edition of 3, private collections

41   Untitled 1995, silkscreen and mixed media 760x500mm, private collection

42   **Victorian Lady** 1995, silkscreen and mixed media 760x700mm

43   Untitled 1995, silkscreen and mixed media 760x700mm

44   Untitled 1990, lino monoprint and collage 250x250mm, private collection

45   Untitled 1996, silkscreen and lino monoprint with solvent transfer 760x700mm

46   Detail of Untitled 1998, vitreous enamel 3.8x45 metres, commissioned by Taylor-Woodrow Properties plc and The Pool of London Partnership, St Katharine Docks, London. Photographer: Simon Marsh

47–49   as above

50   Untitled 1995, vitreous enamel 2000x750mm, commissioned by Look Ahead Housing Association Ltd, Aldegate Hostel, (Beacon House), London

51   Untitled 1998, oil on screenprint 1000x760mm, private collection

52   Untitled notebook drawing 1997, 150x100mm

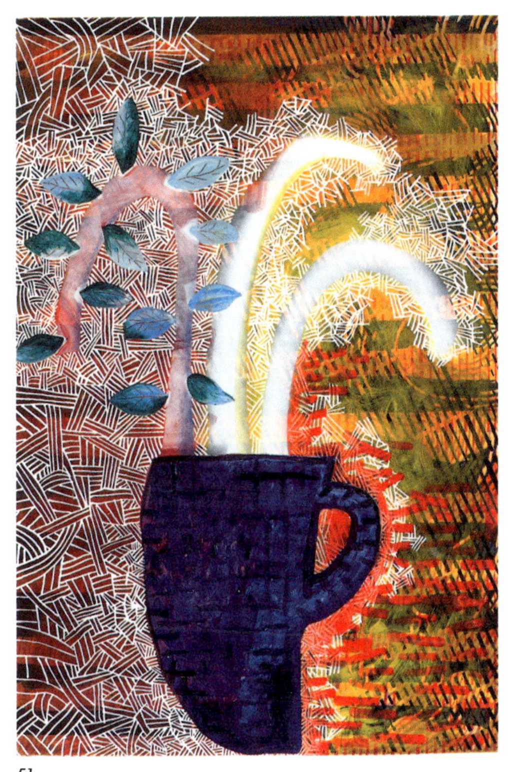

51

Dale Devereux Barker

1962	Born, Leicester
1984-86	Slade School of Fine Art, London
1984	Cyprus College of Art, Paphos, Cyprus
1981-84	Leicester Polytechnic School of Fine Art
1980-81	Loughborough College of Art and Design

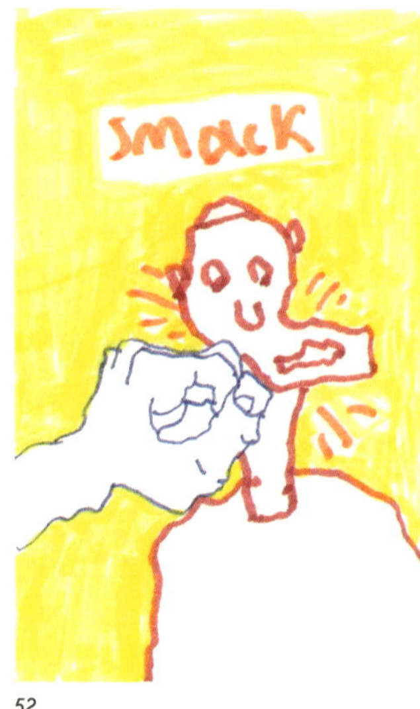

52

Solo Exhibitions

2000	EXCESSIVE PLEASURES **Firstsite, Minories Art Gallery**, Colchester, Essex
1999	THE HAZARDS OF IMAGERY, **The Eagle Gallery**, London
	RECENT DECENT, **The Chappel Galleries**, Essex
	A LITTLE CLOSE CALLED PARADISE **Buckinghamshire County Museum**
1997	**The Box Gallery**, Tattingstone, Suffolk
	Zella Gallery, London
1996	**The Earl of Smith Gallery**, Leamington Spa
	Printworks, Colchester, Essex
	COME UPSTAIRS AND SEE MY ETCHINGS 'The Room Upstairs', **Christchurch Mansion**, Ipswich
1995	A RETROSPECTIVE, **The Fermoy Arts Centre**, Kings Lynn, Norfolk
	A DECADE OF PRINTMAKING, **Clifford Chance**, Little Britain, London
1994	IN DEFENCE OF THE PLEASURE PRINCIPLE, **Jill George Gallery**, London
	Printworks, Colchester, Essex
1993	**John Russell Gallery**, Ipswich, Suffolk
1992	UNIQUE STATE, **Jill George Gallery**, London
1991	**Printworks**, Colchester, Essex
	Landsberg Museum, Landsberg, Bavaria, Germany
	THE DREAMING SIDE, **The Eagle Gallery**, London
1990	**Gainsborough's House**, Sudbury, Suffolk
1989	LEAVES TO FIND, **Galerie Dusseldorf**, Perth, Western Australia

Two Man Exhibitions

1998	**Bircham Gallery, Kings Lynn** (with John Pollex)
1996	**Jill George Gallery**, London (with Mark Francis)
1995	**120 Old Broad Street**, London (with Lee Grandjean)
1991	**Harlow Theatre**, Collaboration with Martin Stannard (Poet)
1988	TWO PRINTMAKERS, **Curwen Gallery**, London (with Chris Bloor)
1985	THE RELIEF OF COINCIDENCE, **Curwen Gallery**, London (with Roy Voss)

Selected Group Exhibitions

1999	12th NORWEGIAN INTERNATIONAL PRINT TRIENNALE
	RELIEF PRINTING TODAY **Gainsborough's House**, Sudbury
	NATIONAL PRINT COMPETITION, Printmakers Council, The Atrium, **Whiteleys**, London
	NO DAY WITHOUT A LINE, **Ashmolean Museum**, Oxford
	TAKEAWAY, **The Red Dot Gallery**, Ipswich
1998	INTERNATIONAL PRINT TRIENNALE, Cracow, Poland and tour, including Museum of Modern Art, Rio de Janeiro, Brazil
	11th INTERNATIONAL TRIENNALE, Estonia
	PREMIO INTERNAZIONALE BIELLA PER L'INCISIONE, Italy
	NATIONAL PRINT EXHIBITION, Mall Galleries, London
1997	ROBERT HORNE PRINTMAKING EXHIBITION, **Tullie House**, Carlisle and tour
	ON THE BORDER Open exhibition selected by Mark Wallinger and Griff Rhys-Jones, **Christchurch Mansion**, Ipswich and **Firstsite, Minories Art Gallery**, Colchester, Essex
	3rd BRITISH INTERNATIONAL MINIATURE PRINT EXHIBITION, **City Art Gallery**, Leicester and tour
	EASTERN OPEN, **Fermoy Arts Centre**, Kings Lynn, Norfolk
	INTERNATIONAL PRINT TRIENNALE, Cracow, Poland

HOT BED: CONTEMPORARY BRITISH PRINTS,
Peter Scott Gallery, Lancaster University
SPECTRUM: BRITISH CONTEMPORARY
PRINTMAKERS, **Ayala Museum**, Manila, Phillipines

1996   **The Walter Thompson Gallery**, London
THE LONDON ARTISTS BOOK FAIR, **Barbican Arts Centre**, London
FAMILIAR FACES IN NEW SPACES, **New Academy Gallery**, London
SHELF-LIFE II, **The Eagle Gallery**, London
NATIONAL PRINT EXHIBITION, **Mall Galleries**, London

1995   EASTERN OPEN, **Fermoy Arts Centre**, Kings Lynn, Norfolk
NO BOUNDARIES, **Vision Network Co Ltd**, Shibuya-ku, Tokyo, Japan
NATIONAL OPEN PRINT COMPETITION, Printmakers Council, The Atrium, **Whiteleys**, London

1994   VAASA INTERNATIONAL PRINT BIENNALE, Finland
2nd HARLECH BIENNALE, Wales

1993   LJUBJANA INTERNATIONAL PRINT BIENNALE, Slovenia (British Arts Council selected representative)
2nd KOCHI INTERNATIONAL PRINT BIENNALE, Japan (Commended)
Galerie Dagmar, London

1991   ROYAL SOCIETY OF PAINTER-PRINTMAKERS OPEN, **Bankside Gallery**, London
EASTERN OPEN, **Fermoy Arts Centre**, Kings Lynn, Norfolk

1990   PORTFOLIO 90, **Curwen Gallery**, London
INTERNATIONAL GRAPHICS SHOW, Stuttgart, West Germany
ARTS IN TOWN, **Wolsey Art Gallery**, **Christchurch Mansion**, Ipswich
11th BRITISH INTERNATIONAL PRINT BIENNALE (BRITAIN, USA AND CANADA), **Cartwright Hall**, Bradford and tour Royal College of Art, London
GROUP SHOW; GALLERY ARTISTS, **Thumb Gallery**, London

1989   International Graphics Art Foundation, MINIATURE PRINT BIENNALE, New York and USA tour

1988   International Graphics Arts Foundation, INTERNATIONAL PRINT BIENNALE II, **John Szoke Gallery**, New York and Connecticut
10th BP BRITISH INTERNATIONAL PRINT BIENNALE (BRITAIN AND AUSTRALIA), **Cartwright Hall**, Bradford and tour; Ipswich, Aberdeen, Cardiff, Edinburgh, Poole, Warwick and London

1987   THE SOUTH BANK PICTURE SHOW, **Royal Festival Hall**, London
International Graphics Arts Foundation, MINIATURE PRINT BIENNALE, New York and Connecticut
FIRST SHOWING - TAKE TWO, **Thumb Gallery**, London
EIGHT BY EIGHT, **Curwen Gallery**, London

1985   DOUBLE ELEPHANT, **Barbican Arts Centre**, London
THE CAMDEN ANNUAL, **Camden Arts Centre**, London
INTERNATIONAL PRINT SHOW, **Landesbank**, Stuttgart, West Germany
THE WHITWORTH YOUNG CONTEMPORARIES, **Whitworth Art Gallery**, Manchester
PRATT/SILVERMINE INTERNATIONAL PRINT EXHIBITION, Connecticut and New York
TRADITION AND INNOVATION, Rank Xerox Travelling Print Show
SPIRIT OF LONDON, **Royal Festival Hall**, London
Contemporary Art Society, ART MARKET, **Smiths Gallery**, London

1984   NEW CONTEMPORARIES, **ICA**, The Mall, London
THE STOWELLS TROPHY, **The Royal Academy**, London
THE TRAVELLING PRINT SHOW, **Mulhouse**, Strasbourg, Breda

1983   NEW CONTEMPORARIES, **ICA**, The Mall, London
THE STOWELLS TROPHY, **The Royal Academy**, London

Teaching

1999-   Visiting lecturer, Leeds Metropolitan University
1998-99   Master Class, Gainsborough's House Print Workshop
1997-99   Visiting Lecturer, Harrogate College of Art and Drama
1996-98   Part-time lecturer, University College, Suffolk
1996   Guest Speaker, New York University, USA
1995-96   Part-time lecturer, Suffolk College; Joint Course Leader
1993-95   Lecturer, Suffolk College; 1994 Foundation Course Leader
1992-99   Workshop Co-ordinator, Gainsborough's House Print workshop, Sudbury
1991-92   Visiting Lecturer, Suffolk College
Visiting Lecturer, North Hertfordshire College
1986-87   Visiting Lecturer, Leicester Polytechnic
1991-92   Visiting Lecturer, Leicester Polytechnic

Residences

1999	The Muir Trust, Buckinghamshire County Museum
1998	St Saviours and St Olave's and St Paul's School, London
1997	Lowick House Printmaking Workshop, Cumbria
	Worlingham Middle School
	Deben High School, Felixstowe
1996	Tattingstone County Primary School
1995	Holbrook High School, Ipswich
1994	Northgate School, Ipswich
1991	Impington College, Cambridge - In conjunction with Kettle's Yard, Text and Image Project
1990	Tattingstone County Primary School, Eastern Arts Artist in Schools Scheme
1989	Crown Pools Complex, Ipswich
	Curtin University of Technology, Perth, Western Australia

Artists Books

1999	*Twenty Titles*
1998	*The Hazards of Imagery* published with poet Paul Violi
	Jumbohemian 747, with Chris Bloor
1996	*Vignettes*, published for SHELF LIFE II
	The Anamorphosis with Paul Violi (from the Pataphysics series no 5 Melbourne, Australia)
1995	*Selected Accidents, Pointless Anecdotes* with Paul Violi
	IO, with poet Kenneth Koch
1992	*From A Recluse To A Roving I Will Go* with poet Martin Stannard
1991	*The Dreaming Side* with Emma Hill
1989	*The Legacy*

Awards

1997	Prontaprint Printmaking Prize, Eastern Open, Kings Lynn
1996	Elected Associate Fellow of The Royal Society of Painter-Printmakers
	Robert Horne Award, National Print Exhibition, Mall Galleries, London
1991	Bentley-Clarke Consultancy - Purchase Prize, Royal Society of Painter-Printmakers Open, London
1990	Forbo-Nairn Prize for best linocut, 11th Bradford Print Biennale
1984	Purchase Prize, East Midlands Hospital Print Show - Shape
1983	Travelling Scholarship, Leicester Polytechnic, Fine Arts Award

Commissions

1999	Penguin Books headquarters, London, 3D print commission
	Abbeygate Estates, Ipswich, vitreous enamel commission
	The Age of Aquarius Ball, Intercontinental Hotel, London, print commission
1997-98	Taylor-Woodrow Properties plc and The Pool of London Partnership, St Katharine Docks, Cloister Walk, London, vitreous enamel commission
1995	Look Ahead Housing Association, Beacon House, London, vitreous enamel commission
	Elton John Aids Foundation, Christies, London, print commission
	Nelsons' Homeopathic Medicines, London, print commission
1994-95	Russell Davies (Container Freight) Ipswich, print commission,
1994	David Kirby Design, print commission
1992	British Rail Freight, print commission
	Clifford Chance, Little Britain, London, vitreous enamel commission
1985-86	Lloyds Building, London, print commission

Reviews

1999	*Art Review* (Winter 1999) - Working under Cover by Emma Hill
	East Anglian Daily Times - Exhibition Review 'Recent Decent' Chappel Galleries
	Printmaking today - Prints and poetry, 'A symbiotic relationship' by Anne Desmet
1998	*The New York Times* - Review of The Royal Society of Painter-printmakers at the Connecticut Graphic Arts Centre
	Art Review - St Katharine Docks commission
	Books as Art by Emma Hill, the Cheltenham Festival of Literature
	Printmaking Today - 145 Front Doors (Autumn) - Review of St Katharine Docks commission
1997	*Enamelling Magazine* (Dec) - Review of enamelling commissions
	Images - Exhibition Feature
	Intercity Magazine - Review of exhibition at Christchurch Mansion
1996	*Images* - Exhibition Feature
	East Anglian Daily Times - Feature
1995	*Printmaking Today - What Daren't you do?* Autumn issue. Article and Interview with Tony Warner
1994	*The Independent* - In Defence of the Pleasure Principle

| 1993 | *East Anglian Daily Times* - Review of residency |
| | *The Expressive Art* - Fred Sedgwick |

1993   *East Anglian Daily Times* - Review of residency
        The Expressive Art - Fred Sedgwick

1992   *Artists Newsletter*, From A Recluse To A Roving
        I Will Go

1991   *The Times Educational Supplement*, Tattingstone
        County Primary School - Review of residency
        Art Review, 11th Bradford Print Biennale at the
        Royal College of Art
        Art Review, Royal Society of Painter-Printmakers
        Open
        Art Review, Printworks, Colchester
        Art Review, The Dreaming Side

1990   Wide Angle Anglia Television, Arts in Town
        Art Review, AD '90

1989   Work featured on 'Seeing and Believing - Art Works',
        BBC Television
        Look East BBC Television, Arts in Town
        Wide Angle Anglia Television, Arts in Town
        Art East, The Legacy
        Art Review, The Legacy
        Graphics World (Sept - Oct)

1988   *Art Review*, 10th Bradford Print Biennale
        Art Review, Art in Bloomsbury
        Art Review, Two Printmakers

1987   Work featured in *Time Out*
        Art Review, First Showing - Take Two
        Art Review, AD '87
        Art Review, At Home With Anthony Dawson

1986   *City Limits*, The Relief of Coincidence
        Art Review, The Relief of Coincidence

Public Collections

Victoria and Albert Museum, London
Buckinghamshire County Museum
Atkinson Gallery, Southport Municipal Collection
Ipswich Museums and Galleries
The Ashmolean Museum, Oxford
Hertfordshire County Council
Essex County Council
Southampton City Art Gallery
Norfolk County Council
Curtin University, Western Australia
St Thomas's Hospital, London
Chesterfield Hospital
Chelsea and Westminster Hospital
British Medical Association
Wakefield Museum
Moorfield Eye Hospital, London
The Legal Aid Board, London

Corporate Collections

Penguin Books
Taylor-Woodrow Properties
The Spectator
Coca Cola Schweppes UK
GE Capital
Courtaulds plc
Nelsons' Homeopathic Medicines
Lloyds Insurance
Allied Irish Bank
Clifford Chance
Strutt and Parker
Merck, Sharpe & Dohme
BMW (UK)
British Rail Freight Division
McDonalds UK
Andersen Consulting
Russell Davies, Container Freight Ltd
IBM
Carlton Television
Pizza Express
British Land

Artists Books in the Collections of:

Cheltenham and Gloucester College of Higher Education
The Centre for British Art, Yale University
The Tate Gallery, London,
The Royal Albert Memorial Museum, Exeter
The London Institute
The National book Collection, Victoria and Albert Museum,
London
University of Central England
Metropolitan University, Manchester
The New York Public Library; Astor, Lenox and Tilden
Foundations and Berg Collection USA
New York University, Fale's Library USA
The Houghton Library, Fogg Art Museum USA
Harvard University USA
The Walpole collection, Yale University USA

Thanks

The artist wishes to thank the following for their
generous help, support and patience, in the
development of the exhibition **Excessive
Pleasures** and the making of this publication:
Katherine Wood and Sarah Lockwood at firstsite;
John Purcell at John Purcell Papers; John Dawson
at John Jones framers; Jenny and Alan Milverton
at MF Frames; Paul and Sue Warren at Warren
Graphics; Paul Douglas at Palladian Press; Dr Neil
Cox, Department of Art History and Theory,
University of Essex; Beryl Scott; Roderick Packe;
Paul Violi; Emma Hill; Stephen Hoskins;
Adam Monaghan and Rebecca Weaver.

Forthcoming exhibitions
of Dale Devereux Barker's work include:

Jill George Gallery London
18 July – 18 August 2000
Buckinghamshire County Museum Aylesbury
February – April 2001

Dale Devereux Barker's work is supported by:

MF Frames Limited
10 St Helens Street
Ipswich
Suffolk
IP4 1HJ
01473 225544

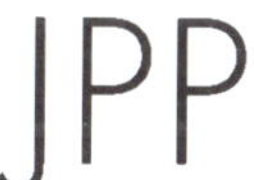

John Purcell Paper
15 Rumsey Road
London
SW9 0TR
0207 737 5199

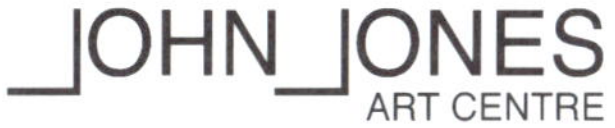

John Jones Art Centre
Stroud Green Road
London N4 3JG
0207 281 5439

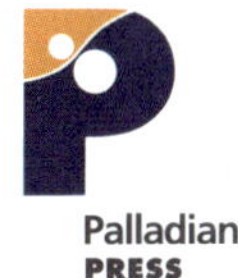

Palladian Press
Unit E
Chandlers Row
Port Lane
Colchester
Essex
CO1 2HG
01206 799065

Published by firstsite
on the occasion of the exhibition

Dale Devereux Barker

Excessive Pleasures

at the Minories Art Gallery · Colchester
January 15 – March 18 2000

This show is dedicated to the memory of Vilma Barker

Firstsite
Director Katherine Wood
74 High Street
Colchester
Essex C01 1UE
Telephone 01206 577067
Fax 01206 577161
Email info@1stsite.keme.co.uk

ISBN 0 948252 06 5

Edited by Katherine Wood

Designed and typeset by Warren Graphics
Produced in England by Palladian Press, Colchester

Paper Neptune Unique · Fenner Paper Company
Edition 2000

Copyright Dale Devereux Barker; Emma Hill; Steve Hoskins;
Adam Monaghan

Photography by Douglas Atfield; Edward Cory; Simon Marsh;
Roderick Packe; Adam Monaghan

Colchester and District Visual Arts Trust trading as firstsite
Registered in England Charity no 1031800

support

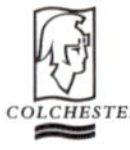
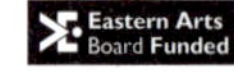

cover image
generated in Apple Works
by the artist 1999